96

Pensionize Your Nest Egg

Pensionize Your Nest Egg

SECOND EDITION

*How to Use Product Allocation to
Create a Guaranteed Income for Life*

Moshe A. Milevsky, PhD
Alexandra C. Macqueen, CFP

WILEY

Cover image: ©iStock.com/xflaunt
Cover design: Wiley

Pensionize™ and Pensionization™ are trademarks of QWeMA Group Inc.

Published by John Wiley & Sons, Inc., Hoboken, New Jersey.

The first edition was published by John Wiley & Sons, Inc. in 2010.

Published simultaneously in Canada.

For general information on our other products and services or for technical support, please contact our Customer Care Department within the United States at (800) 762-2974, outside the United States at (317) 572-3993, or fax (317) 572-4002.

Wiley publishes in a variety of print and electronic formats and by print-on-demand. Some material included with standard print versions of this book may not be included in e-books or in print-on-demand. If this book refers to media such as a CD or DVD that is not included in the version you purchased, you may download this material at http:// booksupport.wiley.com. For more information about Wiley products, visit www.wiley.com.

ISBN 9781119025252 (Hardcover)
ISBN 9781119025283 (ePDF)
ISBN 9781119025276 (ePub)

Printed in the United States of America.

10 9 8 7 6 5 4 3 2 1

Contents

List of Exhibits

Preface

Preface to the Second Edition

The first edition of this book was published in 2010 and covered the Canadian market. We wrote it because we felt, both then and now, that Canadians preparing for retirement needed a clear and better understanding of both the risks they (and their finances) face, and how a "true pension" can help protect retirees from those risks. In the first edition, we provided some step-by-step guides on how to use the new approach of product allocation to protect against the new risks of retirement, and obtain a true pension.

As soon as that first (Canadian) edition was published, we started to get inquiries from prospective retirees in other countries asking how the tools and perspectives of pensionizing could help them, too. Our standard response, for several years, was, "Just refer to the Canadian edition; the terms might be different, but the pension landscape and the math and concepts of pensionizing are pretty much the same...."

We were wrong.

As it turns out, the need for pensionization in the United States, the United Kingdom, Australia, and New Zealand is much more acute than it ever has been in Canada. What we refer to as "true pensions"—employer-provided, workplace pensions that provide a "retirement paycheck" to replace your workplace paycheck at retirement, for as long as you live—are more threatened and have experienced much more significant decline in these countries than in Canada … and that's when they've even been available at all.

At the same time, in the years since the publication of the first edition, successive waves of reform have transformed pension systems in all of these economies—and those transformations are not yet over.

For the past decade, pension reform has been high on the agenda of many governments; with the financial crisis, starting in 2008, only accelerating the pace of change. Pension observers around the world suggest that by now it is widely accepted in most countries that pension systems and rules need to change over time. However, how and where does that leave retirees, who must plan for a safe and secure retirement in an era of profound change, including the dramatic decline of workplace pensions and faltering economic markets?

This revised edition of *Pensionize Your Nest Egg* is our response to that question. We've updated, expanded, and revised the materials inside to cover retirees in the United States, the United Kingdom, Canada, Australia, and New Zealand (a group that we refer to as our "focus areas" or "focus regions"). If you live in one of these places and you're thinking about retirement, this book is for you.

One note before you move forward: because we've covering five regions, there are times we use generic terms instead of country-specific terms. The most obvious instance is the use of "dollars" to refer to currency amounts throughout the book—instead of the pound, for example. However, please note that none of our arguments are based on currency values. Where you see "dollars," you can happily read that as "pounds," if you like, in order to make it more personally relevant to you.

Preface to the First Edition

We're going to ask you to do a lot of speculating, imagining, forecasting, and projecting in this book—and we're going to start now.

We're going to open this book with a fable about a hero on a daring quest.

Let's imagine that hero is you. Your quest is to survive a perilous journey while amassing enough gold pieces to sustain you for the rest of your life, once you've reached the journey's end.

So far, you've traveled many miles over sometimes treacherous ground, following the path through unexpected twists and turns. And you've been gathering gold pieces along the way, carefully storing them in what you hope are safe havens that you can access once your journey is over.

The good news is that the end of your journey is in sight. The bad news is that the danger is not over.

Three new risks have emerged from the shadows, standing between you and the caves where you've stored your gold. Let's get a closer look at them: there's the Dragon of Decaying Currency—will it cause your gold to lose its value over time? What about the dreaded Serpent of the Sequence of Returns— will it unexpectedly make off with half of your fortune? And, finally, does the Specter of Longevity Risk loom over you, rendering you paralyzed with worry about running out of gold while you are still alive?

This book is all about getting you past those mythical beasts— and the very real risks they represent—to your ultimate goal: your safe and happy retirement, free from worry about having enough gold to last for the rest of your days.

In this book, we're going to equip you with all kinds of tools, from special glasses to crafty calculators and more, and these will all help you along the way. But to get you to your goal, we're going to give you a powerful shield—one that can vanquish the beasts we've just described while protecting your gold for as long as you live. That shield is pensionization.

What is "pensionization"? It is the process of taking a fraction of your nest egg (your hoard of stored gold) and turning it into a guaranteed income that lasts for your lifetime. Pensionizing your nest egg enables you to get where you need to go. It will ensure you have enough income (enough gold pieces) for as long as you need it.

The truth is: your nest egg is probably more fragile than you think, and the strategies you've used to protect yourself up until now won't be sufficient as you move into and through retirement.

In the coming pages, we will examine the new risks you and your nest egg face in retirement, and we'll lay the groundwork for you to safeguard yourself and your financial fortunes.

How to Use This Book

So is this book for you? Well, it isn't a forum to complain about the state of public policy for those entering retirement. It isn't a platform to agitate for particular changes to retirement income programs. Nor is it a budgeting book providing tips and tricks about how to save more and spend less. It isn't a retirement planning book with quizzes about your psychological readiness to leave the world of work, or a financial planning book with tables that help you calculate the required withdrawals from your retirement savings accounts over time.

Instead, this is a book designed for all the "pension-poor" future (and present) retirees who want, need, and demand a plan to create pension-like income that will sustain them for the rest of their lives. It is your personal tool kit to pensionize your nest egg.

Sound good? If so, here's how to use the rest of this book:

- Part One focuses on why you need to build your own pension plan. It includes an overview of the real pension challenges in the United States, the United Kingdom, Canada, Australia, and New Zealand—and the challenges you will face as you ready yourself for the retirement stage of life. You'll learn why asset allocation and other time-honored rules for building savings on the way to this milestone all fall short when it comes time to convert your savings into a stream of income for the rest of your life. Read this part to see exactly what new risks you need to protect yourself against as you reach retirement, and why.

- Part Two introduces the modern solution to securing retirement income (actually, the solution is hundreds of years old). Read this part to understand how product allocation differs from asset allocation, to explore the theoretical arguments for creating a personal pension in retirement, and to get an up-to-date overview of the financial products that are available to help you to pensionize your nest egg.

- Part Three shows you the step-by-step process you need to follow to convert your nest egg into a guaranteed stream of income for the rest of your life. Complete with illustrations and examples, this chapter gives you the tools you need to create your own personal pensionized income. Read this part to learn how to design a plan that works for you and your life.

One more note before we get started: when reading this book, you will encounter two authors from completely different backgrounds. One is a professor (in the business, finance, and math fields), and one is a practicing financial planner. Occasionally, you might read something and think, "What the heck was that about?" Those are probably the parts where the math prof got the upper hand. Don't worry; we will always bring you back to reality (or at least one of us will!). This book is designed to be read and understood by ordinary retirees and those preparing for retirement, whether you are working through it on your own or talking the ideas through with your financial adviser.

Are you ready? Let's begin.

Introduction

Why Retirement Income Is Better than Retirement Savings

It is early September in the year 2045, and Gertrude has just turned 85 years old. She is in relatively good health and is enjoying this quiet, uncomplicated stage of her life. She has time for her hobbies, which include membership in her local gardening society and a regular poker night with friends, and time for her family, who visit most holidays and indulge her on birthdays. Her everyday companions include her small dog, Perky, and the young dog walker she has hired to provide the daily activity Perky needs to keep fit. (Running around the park is a little beyond Gertrude these days.)

Gertrude's income (all in 2015 dollars) consists of about $10,000 per year in an old-age government pension, about $7,000 in dividends, and an additional $40,000 from an indexed life annuity she purchased from an insurance company many years ago. While she doesn't have much in the way of investments, she does have a financial adviser to manage her small stock and bond portfolio. Mainly, they talk about how much Gertrude wants to donate to charity each year. In fact, the only money question Gertrude really has to deal with is how to spend the annual income of $50,000 that she receives from her pension and life annuities.

Given her family history, Gertrude worries about Alzheimer's, and she does her best to keep herself mentally and physically active by assembling the puzzles she downloads and prints on her home 3-D printer, and with trips to the local swimming pool. She has a social network of friends, and the topic of money is rarely discussed. Certainly, Gertrude never brings it up—she decided long ago that she didn't want to spend the rest of her life worrying about these things. That's why she chose, as she was preparing for retirement, to pensionize her retirement savings nest egg by converting some of her savings into a stream of income she couldn't outlive.

Contrast this tranquil picture with another possible future for Gertrude: Gertrude has recently celebrated her 85th birthday. While she is happy to have reached this age, her life is not worry-free—she feels stressed and uncertain about the daily financial decisions she needs to make. Even a seemingly simple choice like whether or not to go ahead with the surgery her beloved Chihuahua requires is not straightforward because Gertrude doesn't know for sure whether the cost of her pet's care will impact her own living expenses.

She does her best to follow the financial papers and the stock markets so she can figure out how much she can withdraw from her portfolio every month, but in the back of her mind she has a rising fear that she's missing important details and making bad decisions. She is also concerned about the cost of her Alzheimer's medication and worries that affordable alternatives may never become available in her lifetime.

Every day, Gertrude tells herself that she will make a better attempt to read the information that her financial adviser sent her about a new product that he feels is right for her. But she's been making this promise for weeks now, and the package is still sitting unopened on her kitchen table.

It is the year 2045 and the mutual funds that she was quite comfortable with back when they existed have been replaced by ZQBs, which are the great-grandkids of the ETFs that were popular in the early part of the 21st century. Gertrude's financial adviser—her fourth in the past three decades (the first two died of heart attacks and the third retired)—mentioned to her the last time they met that she might have to reduce her spending from the portfolio because of the great timber market crash of 2037, which caused ZQB yields to contango into backwardation. (Or was it the other way around? She can't quite remember.)

Gertrude's husband, Harry, who passed away a few years ago, always used to handle money issues for both of them. Harry left quite a bit of money to Gertrude, but no instruction manual. Her adviser said these decisions are up to her (and not him), but Gertrude hates thinking about these increasingly complicated financial issues. Her friends don't seem interested in talking about money, so she is relying more and more on her financial adviser for his advice. But she only sees or talks to him every few months, and he's not available in the late-night moments when she is most worried about keeping everything together.

Gertrude would love to spend more time doing the things she enjoys—like keeping up with her favorite TV broadcasts on her holographic wristwatch TV and maintaining correspondence with her far-flung extended family—but she doesn't feel able to relax enough to truly enjoy life. Should she go ahead with surgery for her dog or not? How much can she take out of her portfolio this year, and next year, and the year after that? Should she buy this newfangled financial product or stick with what she already has? Will she ever be able to ignore the financial news, or will she need to open envelopes full of scary and confusing information for the rest of her life?

Parallel Gertrudes: which one is better off? We believe your answer is the same as ours: Gertrude 1 wins. In fact, extensive studies by psychologists have shown that Gertrude 1 is happier than Gertrude 2.

This book is all about making sure "your Gertrude"—that is, your future self—has plenty of income, as opposed to enough money. So how did Gertrude 1 come out ahead? Easy: she pensionized her nest egg. Twenty years ago she made some smart decisions that converted a fraction of her nest egg into income she can't outlive. As a result, she not only has all the income she needs, she also has a worry-free life. In contrast, aiming to have "enough money" gives you the problems of Gertrude 2.

Not sure about the difference? Read on to learn everything you need to know about creating your own guaranteed income for life.

TECHNICAL GLOSSARY

Here is a basic refresher on some of the terms you will encounter as you make your way through this book, in case you need refreshing.

Averages and Means, Geometric and Arithmetic:
As you read through this book, you will find a couple of places in which we refer to *averages* and *means*, and even *geometric* and *arithmetic* averages and means.

The term "average" is usually used to mean the arithmetic average. The arithmetic average of a set of numbers is the sum of all the numbers in the set, divided by the amount of numbers in the set. If you wanted to find, for example, the average score that a group of students achieved on a test, you would add all of the test scores and then divide by the number of students in the class. The resulting number is the arithmetic average, which is the same as its *mean*; the two terms are synonyms.

But there are some instances, especially in the world of finance, where an arithmetic mean is not an appropriate method for calculating an average.

Suppose you have an investment that earns 12 percent the first year, 40 percent the second year, and 20 percent the third year. What is its average rate of return? In this case, in the first year your investment was *multiplied by* (not added to) 1.12, in the second year it was multiplied by 1.40, and in the third year it was multiplied by 1.20.

In this case, we know that we cannot use the arithmetic mean, because that adds the values in a set. Instead, we need to use the *geometric mean* (or geometric average), which is the *product* of these values—the result of multiplying these numbers.

The geometric mean identifies the central tendency or typical value of a set of numbers by using the product of their values, not the sum of their values. It is useful anytime you are working with groups of values that are multiplicative, such as the calculation of investment returns on a portfolio over time.

Expected Values:
In statistics and probability analysis, an expected value is calculated by multiplying each possible outcome by the likelihood that each outcome will occur, and adding together all of those values. The expected value is thus the *probability-weighted average of all possible values*.

(*continued*)

real
returns

Real and Nominal Values:

Throughout this book, you will find a few mentions of "real" returns or what something is worth in "real" terms. In finance and economics, a real value is one that has been adjusted to remove the effects of inflation. For example, if you earn 2 percent from a bank deposit and inflation is also 2 percent, you are left with nothing real!

Standard Deviation:

In statistics and probability theory, the standard deviation measures the amount of variation or dispersion from the average (in the examples in this book, from the arithmetic mean).

A low standard deviation indicates that the data points tend to be very close to the mean; a high standard deviation indicates that the data points are spread out over a large range of values.

Why You Need to Build Your Own Pension Plan:

The Most Predictable Crisis in History

1

The Real Pension Crisis

The Wall Street Journal (United States), October 6, 2014—Pension Dropouts Cause Pinch: "Motorola Solutions Inc. and Bristol-Myers Squibb Co. are the latest companies to cast off billions in pension burdens, fueling a trend that could weaken the government's ability to protect the payouts other employers have promised millions of retired workers. … Only 14 percent of the nation's private-sector workers were covered by defined benefit plans in 2011, less than half the 38 percent in 1979. …"

The Guardian (U.K.), February 22, 2013—Pension scheme membership at 15-year low: "Membership of workplace pension schemes fell for the 11th year running in 2012, to 46% of the British workforce, official figures have shown … Defined benefit pension schemes, also known as final salary, continue to disappear from workplaces … The figures show that 91% of public sector employees with workplace pensions had a final salary scheme in 2012, against just 26% in the private sector."

The Globe and Mail (Canada), February 20, 2014—Shift from defined benefit pensions reinforces need for retirement planning: "For decades, most workers relied on a promise of how much they would receive in retirement from their company pensions. … But that pension certainty is fading as many companies—faced with large unfunded liabilities and deficits amid low interest rates—moved employees, especially new recruits, to defined contribution plans that guarantee contributions but not final monthly pensions."

The Sunday Morning Herald (Australia), May 10, 2014—Superannuation well managed could avert a huge blowout on pensions: "A recent report by CPA Australia, based on analysis of more than 8,000 households across the nation, claims Boomers—those born between 1946 and 1965—are using super savings as a windfall to prop up lifestyles during their working lives rather than as an investment to be nurtured for the 25 years of retirement expected for the average person reaching 65 years. According to the Actuaries Institute, most people's superannuation account balances are increasing but will not be enough to meet even a modest lifestyle, regardless of whether it is paid out as a lump sum, converted to an income stream, or ploughed into other investments."

The New Zealand Herald, May 9, 2014—Private pensions for the lucky few: "Today, 1 in 10 retired people have an income stream from an occupational pension. … However, by the time today's 48-year-old arrives at retirement, the number getting any private pension at all will be very few, let alone pensions that are inflation protected. … What will today's 48-year-old do when she reaches retirement in 2031? How will she make her nest egg last?"

Chances are, if you picked up a newspaper over the past few months, or even years, you saw many alarming articles reporting on the dire state of retirement income systems throughout the regions we are focusing on in this book: the United States, the United Kingdom, Canada, Australia, and New Zealand. Flipping through the pages of your morning newspaper, you can find facts, figures, and commentary on the declining place of pensions in these countries, along with lots of agreement about the need for changes, or discussion about changes that are already taking place. Right now, there's an active debate about the future of pensions around the world. We are awash in expert commissions, opinions from public-policy think tanks, and calls for reform from ordinary citizens and voters. But what's the crisis? Why the need for reform? What reform is needed? And what difference does any of this make for you?

Up a Creek without a Pension Paddle

The recent, and very public, debate about the safety of retirement income is replete with startling statistics. In particular, reports quoted by all participants in the discussion note the declining rates of participation in employer-sponsored occupational or workplace pension plans. So let's review what belonging to this kind of pension plan means for those who participate. The common understanding is that if you participate in a workplace pension plan, when you retire, your "work paycheck" will seamlessly convert to a "retirement paycheck" that you'll receive for the rest of your life (which means that your relationship with your employer never really ends, as long as you are alive).

The unspoken implication of these discussions, of course, is that people without an employer-sponsored pension are "up a creek … without a pension paddle." In contrast to the lucky population with employer-sponsored pensions, they will be living on cat food in retirement, counting every penny as the days go by, and constantly fretting about outliving their savings (or if they aren't worried, they should be!).

At first glance, the available data seem to support this rather bleak picture. Let's take a look at the pension landscape in the countries where we are focusing our attention:

- In the United States, only 45 percent of the workforce is covered by an employer-sponsored pension plan.

- In the United Kingdom, front-page stories in 2012 announced that the proportion of U.K. workers enrolled in workplace pensions had fallen below 50 percent.

- In Canada, statistics show that a mere 33 percent of the Canadian labor force participated in a registered pension plan in 2012.

- In Australia, the introduction of compulsory superannuation (government-sponsored workplace pension plans) has led to the closure of many of the employer-sponsored pension plans that existed before superannuation: in 1995, there were approximately 4,200 plans, but by 2010, only 168 remained.

- And in New Zealand, coverage of occupational pension plans has been falling over time: the ratio of workers in employer-sponsored pension plans as a percentage of the employed workforce fell from almost 14 percent in 2003 to just over 10 percent in 2011, while in June 2012 the number of people enrolled in KiwiSaver accounts—voluntary long-term savings accounts intended for retirement—was equal to roughly 34 percent of the working-age population.

Ergo, it is no surprise that the public policy question *du jour* is what to do about those people who aren't fortunate enough, or savvy enough, to participate in employer-sponsored workplace pension plans over the course of their careers. Surely, conventional wisdom suggests, these are the people most at risk of inadequate retirement savings.

Mixing Defined Benefit Apples and Defined Contribution Oranges

But allow us to be contrarians for a moment. We are actually quite concerned not just for those people with no employer-sponsored pension plan, but also for a large fraction of the so-called "lucky" workers—those who think they will retire to a guaranteed pension income, when in fact they have nothing of the sort.

To understand this concern, we need to examine what we mean when we talk about pensions. If you are among the people contemplating retirement in the next decade, cast your memory back to what the world of work was like when you first joined it. Thirty years ago, many of the largest employers in North America and the United Kingdom offered what are known as defined benefit (DB) pensions to their employees. These are voluntary, occupational pension plans (in that their establishment is voluntary, not mandatory, for employers—who are the sponsors of the plans, while employees are the beneficiaries). This form of pension promises a lifetime of income to each retiree when he or she stops working, with the potential for a survivor pension for your spouse after you die, too. Note our emphasis on "promise" and "lifetime of income"—these are key distinctions in the world of pensions. If you started work for a large company 30 years ago in North America or the United Kingdom, chances are pretty good that you have a DB pension plan.

But over the past few decades, the proportion of companies offering DB pensions to new employees has steadily dropped. Today, if you work in the public sector, chances are you (still) have a DB pension plan. But if you work in the private sector, your chances aren't so good—if you have a pension plan, it is likely a defined contribution (DC) plan, also known as a money purchase plan (or you may have a hybrid or "target benefit" plan, both of which mix elements of DB and DC pensions—see Exhibit 1.1 for an overview of the differences between the various kinds of pension plans). Now, DC pensions are still considered pension plans for statistical or census purposes, so people who participate in DC plans are typically counted in the "lucky" group of participants who belong to a registered pension plan.

However, DC pensions, despite their name, are essentially nothing more than tax-sheltered investment plans and offer no promises

Exhibit 1.1 Defined Benefit versus Defined Contribution, Hybrid, and Target Benefit Pension Plans

Defined Benefit	Defined Contribution	Hybrid	Target Benefit
Income is determined by a formula based on earnings history and years of service	Income is determined by the amount the employee contributed, the amount the employer contributes, proper investment selection, and market performance	Income is determined by a mix of DB and DC elements	Income is determined by a formula, but is not guaranteed
Example: the payout during retirement equals 2% x years of service x final salary	Example: the employee contributes 5% of salary and the employer contributes 5%	The DB component provides a guaranteed minimum benefit or "floor," with top-ups tied to a DC account	Employer and employee contributions are fixed according to a predetermined rate or formula that is expected to be sufficient to fund benefits according to a DB-like formula (the target benefit)
The employer guarantees a certain benefit level at retirement	No guaranteed benefit at retirement	The employer guarantees the DB component, while the DC component is not guaranteed	No guaranteed benefit at retirement

Defined Benefit	Defined Contribution	Hybrid	Target Benefit
The employer absorbs all the financial and demographic risk	The employee absorbs all the financial and demographic risk	Risk is shared between employers and employees; with the risk for the DB component borne by the employer and the risk for the DC component absorbed by the employee	Risk is shared between employers and employees, and benefits can be reduced if the plan experiences a deficit—or employer and employees can opt to increase contributions
The employer is responsible for paying the pension benefits	The employer has no responsibility beyond the retirement date	The employer is responsible for paying the pension benefits tied to the DB component only	Accumulated benefits can be increased or reduced if the funded status of the plan changes, or employee contributions can be increased (or contribution increases can be split with the employer)

of lifetime income. Here's the difference between the two kinds of pension plans: in a defined contribution plan, the amounts contributed to the plan are known. In a defined benefit plan, the amounts paid out of the plan (the benefits) are known and guaranteed. In a DB plan, certainty comes after retirement. In a DC plan, the only certainty is before retirement.

UNDERSTANDING PENSIONS: A PENSION GLOSSARY

Part of the difficulty in understanding the "pension crisis" around the world is the lack of a common vocabulary for pension issues.

The Organization for Economic Cooperation and Development's (OECD) Working Party on Private Pensions has developed a pensions classification and glossary to help ensure basic terminology is shared by OECD members. The Working Party created a set of pension classifications, which we are including here, as they can help readers think through the concepts we are discussing in this book.

Public versus Private
Pension plans can be *public* (administered by the general government, such as a central state or local government, as well as other public-sector bodies such as Social Security institutions), or they can be *private* (administered by institutions other than government). "Social Security" or "old-age" pensions are examples of public pension plans.

Occupational versus Personal
Within the private pension plan category, pensions can be *occupational* (access to these pensions is linked to your employment) or *personal* (plans are not linked to employers).

Mandatory versus Voluntary

Within both the occupational and personal pension plan categories, pensions can be *mandatory* for employers (employers are obliged by law to participate in a pension plan), or *voluntary* (employers can choose whether or not to establish an employee pension plan).

Defined Contribution versus Defined Benefit

Finally, within the occupational pension plan category, pensions can be *defined contribution* plans, for which the employer pays fixed or set contributions and has no obligation to pay further contributions to an ongoing plan in the event of unfavorable plan experience, or *defined benefit* plans, where benefits are typically linked to the employee's wages or salary, length of employment, or other factors.

What Is a True Pension?

In this book, when we discuss the decline of "true pensions," we are referring to *private, occupational, voluntary, defined benefit pension plans*. These are pensions established voluntarily by employers and providing a defined benefit in retirement, for as long as you live. These pensions provide a promise that you—the retiree—will receive a real, predictable, and reliable income stream for the rest of your natural life.

In defined contribution pension plans, funds flow into the pension plan from the employer, the employee, or both, are invested in the volatile stock and bond markets, and the gains are tax deferred until the income is received—but nowhere is there any mention of a guarantee. There's no promise of lifetime income. Instead, your retirement future is subject to the random ups and downs of the stock and bond

Exhibit 1.2 Who Has a True Pension?

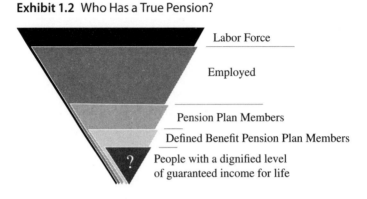

markets. (In Chapter 3, you'll learn exactly how risky it is to leave the security of your retirement income to the whims of the markets.)

So, given this insight into the differing kinds of pensions available today, let's look again at how many people will retire from the workforce with a true pension.

Exhibit 1.2 provides a way to think about this issue and where you fit in the pension landscape: do you have a "true pension" or not?

THE DECLINE OF TRUE PENSIONS: AN OVERVIEW

Pension systems in all of the regions we are focusing on have changed since the financial crisis. These reforms followed an earlier wave of changes implemented in the previous decade. Here's an overview of the current pension landscape in each region (detailed sources are available in the Notes).

The United States
In 1989, approximately 60 percent of the employed population had pension coverage of one kind or another, with the proportion of defined benefit to defined contribution plans split close to equally.

In 2013 (the latest year for which data are available), 46 percent of American workers aged 21 to 64 participated in an employer-sponsored pension plan—but only 26 percent participated in a defined benefit pension, with the remainder in defined contribution plans. And of the workers participating in defined benefit plans, more than one in two are in the public sector.

The United Kingdom

The role of the defined benefit pension in the United Kingdom has diminished drastically since the year 2000, especially in the private sector. The decline has been so steep that many observers believe that the defined benefit plan "cannot survive as an institution" in the private sector.

Across the United Kingdom in 2013, there were a total of 8.1 million people enrolled in voluntary occupational pension plans—the lowest level since the 1950s.

For both DB and DC occupational pensions, in 2013, just under two thirds of membership (65 percent, or 5.3 million) was in the public sector and just over one third (34 percent, or 2.8 million) was in the private sector. This is in contrast to 1953 (when the pension survey from which these data are taken was first run), when active membership of occupational schemes was divided equally between the private and public sectors.

For the younger generation, the option of joining a DB scheme is much reduced. In 2013, only 38 percent of DB plans were open to new members. In 2014, the number of active participants in DC plans outnumbered active participants in DB plans.

The United Kingdom is now undertaking a major reform of its pension system. In October 2012, the government began

(continued)

rolling out automatic enrollment into workplace pension schemes. Once complete (in February 2018), all employers will have a legal duty to enroll all qualifying workers in a workplace pension plan, which can be either defined contribution or defined benefit. To support automatic enrollment, the government has also established the National Employment Savings Trust (NEST), a trust-based occupational defined contribution scheme.

And, most recently, in March 2014 the requirement that U.K. residents must purchase an annuity with DC pension savings by the age of 75 was removed. Options for accessing savings in DC pensions now include withdrawing funds over time or as a lump sum, in addition to annuitizing.

Canada

In Canada, steady public sector employment growth, where DB pension coverage is nearly universal, has partially obscured the large decline in voluntary occupational pension coverage in private-sector employment over the past decade.

In 2012, a total of 33 percent of the Canadian labor force was enrolled in a registered pension plan, a proportion that is unchanged since 2002. Eighty-six percent of public-sector workers are enrolled in a registered pension plan (again, a figure unchanged since 2002), but the proportion of private-sector workers covered by a pension plan declined from 27 percent in 2002 to 24 percent in 2012.

At the same time, the proportion of public-sector workers enrolled in a DB pension plan increased from 2002 to 2012, from 93 to 94 percent, while the proportion of private-sector workers with DB plans fell dramatically, from 73 to 48 percent—and where DB plans exist in the private sector, most new employees are not offered membership in DB plans.

A recent survey of retirement readiness found a strong majority of Canadians—approximately 80 percent—are financially prepared for retirement. However, the survey found that those who are least prepared for retirement are middle- to high-income households who either have access to employer-sponsored retirement savings vehicles but don't contribute enough to these plans, or don't have access to an employer plan and have below-average personal retirement savings.

Australia

In Australia, the advent of compulsory superannuation, a mandatory employer contribution to a private pension plan, in 1992 prompted the closure of many employer-sponsored pension plans. Twenty years ago, in 1995, there were slightly over 4,200 employer-sponsored plans; by 2010, that number had fallen to just 168.

Today, the Australian employer-provided pension system stands out from other industrial country systems for two reasons: first, coverage has more than doubled over the past 25 years (among people who are employed, coverage is close to universal); and second, the dominant kind of pension plan is now defined contribution, not defined benefit.

At retirement age, members of a superannuation plan can withdraw the accumulated capital as a lump sum or as an income stream. Currently, most benefits are taken as a lump sum (at least in part), and the pensions industry in Australia is now grappling with the question of how lifetime income in retirement can be generated from these plans.

(*continued*)

New Zealand

New Zealand is home to the first nationwide auto-enrollment retirement savings plan in the 34 countries of the OECD. "KiwiSaver" retirement savings accounts were introduced in 2007 and have been highly effective in ensuring high participation rates among new employees, due to the automatic enrollment feature (which requires participants to opt out).

Today, about 55 percent of workers in New Zealand are enrolled in KiwiSaver accounts. KiwiSaver entitles members to a lump sum, not a pension, on withdrawal at age 65 or over.

Prior to the development of the national KiwiSaver program, less than 10 percent of the population of New Zealand had access to a company-sponsored pension plan.

It Takes Two to Tango: A Basic Lesson about the Nature of True Pensions

In short, the current public discussion of the pension crisis in our focus regions glosses over the vital distinction between DB and DC pensions. Today, the term *pension* is used to describe both DB and DC pension plans (as well as hybrid and target-date plans), with the result that many people who think they have a pension are really members of a collective saving and investment plan or a capital accumulation plan, such as a defined contribution pension plan or a profit-sharing plan.

So let's be perfectly clear about what we mean when we talk about pensions in this book. A pension is not a synonym for a large sum of money, diversified asset allocation, or a retirement residence in Florida, Portugal, or Bali. In our view, even a seven-figure 401(k), NEST, Registered Retirement Savings Plan (RRSP), MySuper, KiwiSaver, or DC pension plan balance is not a pension.

Instead, a pension involves a binding contract. A pension includes a guarantee. A pension is a pledge that you—the retiree—will receive a real, predictable, and reliable income stream for the rest of your natural life. A pension is more than an asset class; it is a product class. (We'll provide lots more information on asset allocation versus product allocation in Part Two. And while the phrase "product allocation" may be new to you now, by the end of this book you'll be an expert in it.)

A true pension also involves more than just you. A true pension tango requires two parties: you, the prospective retiree, and your dance partner, the entity standing behind the promise. The counterparty to the pension promise can be an insurance company, government entity, or corporate pension plan. But for it to be called a genuine pension there must be somebody guaranteeing something. No guarantee? No pension.

Guarantee versus Ruin

You may be asking: "Why is a guarantee so important?" The answer is very basic. Our quantitative analysis indicates that a prospective retiree—who could be you—might have 20, 30, or even 40 times their annual income needs in investable wealth (what we would call a wealth-to-needs ratio of 20, 30, or 40; more on this ratio later). These assets could be sitting in the most diversified of mutual funds, investments, retirement savings accounts, or even in a DC pension plan, and yet the retiree still runs the risk that the portfolio will not last as long as he or she does. This is the nature of random and unpredictable human longevity combined with financial volatility. In the language of retirement income planning, retirement income streams without guarantees are subject to a high "lifetime ruin probability"—which happens when you are alive but your portfolio is dead.

Ironically, both good news (future breakthroughs in medical science) and bad news (unexpected personal inflation or another miserable decade in the stock market) can negatively affect your income prospects in retirement. That is, events on either side of the ledger can wreak havoc on the retirements of even the wealthiest of retirees. (We'll be talking about these kinds of risks in Chapters 2 through 4.)

When Is a Pension Not a Pension?

You may be thinking: "I have a true pension—the DB kind—so I'm free and clear of worry." But are you?

As we've said, if you have a guaranteed lifetime pension, your pension dance partner is supposed to continue to send your monthly checks, come economic hell or financial high water. Note that this is no trivial promise to make. However, as illustrated in the opening to this chapter, many corporations—from United Airlines to Nortel Networks—have defaulted or are in the process of weaseling out of their simple contracts. Others have given their aging pensioners undesirable financial haircuts by reducing their expected monthly income after the fact. In the past few decades, companies have walked away from pension obligations and dumped the problem on governments and the public. Retiring employees, who expected a seamless transition from work paycheck to retirement paycheck, are instead spending their (unpaid!) time battling with former employers about the status of their pension claims. Their promised pensions failed to materialize—their pension partners walked off the dance floor.

Today, a true pension is as rare as it is expensive. We think even the promise of a gold-plated corporate DB pension paying 100 percent of pre-retirement salary, inflation adjusted for the rest of the retiree's life, is not a pension if the company can renege on the promise by filing for bankruptcy. Today, stories from Detroit and Illinois in the United States demonstrate how even seemingly secure state-backed pensions can be vulnerable, as pensioners and future retirees emerge from years of political wrangling, insolvency proceedings, and legislative rulings with scaled-back retirement pensions.

There Ain't No Such Thing … as a Free Pension

Now that we've given a sense of the personal value of a true pension, let's talk about the cost.

To get an idea of what a true guaranteed pension will set you back these days, consider the following example. Imagine you're a 62-year-old contemplating retirement. You ask your favorite A-rated insurance company agent to provide a quote for a personal pension. They offer something in the following price range: for every $10,000 of guaranteed annual income you would like to receive for the rest of your life, you must give us $211,500 up front (in early 2015, using market rates). Yes, you read that correctly: you need to ante up with more than twenty times the desired annual income. So let's do the math. If you want $50,000 of annual income with an annual cost of living adjustment of 2 percent for the rest of your life, that'll cost you about a cool million. No, this is no Madoff-like scheme to make off with your retirement savings account—this is the fair price in the open market for an indexed life annuity, which is the closest thing to a DB pension that exists in the retail market. If this type of retirement income seems too expensive, the market price is telling you something about what true pensions are actually worth. (In later chapters, we'll talk in more detail about the costs of your own, self-purchased pension, including how external variables, such as the inflation rate, affect the amount you can expect to receive.)

Now, you might decide, "Heck, I have $1 million in retirement savings and I can invest it myself to create my own $50,000 pension." Well, here is our warning to you: There is no risk-free lunch. There is a very good reason the insurance company charges you what seems to be so much. First, interest rates are abnormally low right now relative to historical rates, and these low rates increase the cost of any guarantee. Second, and more importantly, by offering you a lifetime income stream, they are taking the risk that you'll outlive your savings off your personal balance sheet—and placing it on their corporate balance sheet. Generating $50,000 per year might not seem like much if you have a million to spare, but if you have that viewpoint, you are probably not seeing the whole picture, and it's time to nudge you back to reality. Pensions are expensive because they are valuable, even if you don't think so.

In fact, according to something called the "life-cycle model of consumption"—which is a marvelous framework used by economists to measure consumer demand for consumption, savings, and investment from cradle to grave—the true value of a true pension is astonishingly high. To understand how the life-cycle model operates, think of it as a bathroom scale. You can use the scale to measure the weight of any item, even if you can't weigh it directly. For example, if you stand on the bathroom scale fully clothed and then do the same totally naked, you can calculate the weight of your clothes even if you never put them directly on the scale.

The model can be used in this way to measure the "utility value," or perceived usefulness, of a pension. To make a long and complex mathematical story short, the utility value of a pension can be worth up to half of your typical net worth. One implication of this finding is that a rational retiree (risk-averse, healthy, and pensionless) would rather have $500,000 worth of pension than $1 million worth of cash, given the choice of only one. Yes, you read that correctly. The message from this model is that most retirees would be willing to pay—keeping in mind that willingness to pay is a fundamental concept in economics—a large premium to exchange their cash for pensions. (We'll delve further into the life-cycle model and how it applies to the world of pensions in Chapter 9.)

The First True Pensions

Back in 1881, the German Chancellor, Otto von Bismarck, introduced the first old-age, state-paid pension and basically invented
defined benefit pensions as we know them today. These old-age
pensions were to be paid by the state to all its elderly citizens. Notice
that he didn't introduce a tax-sheltered savings plan or create some
group DC plan. Bismarck's intentions, instead, were to collectively
force children to care for their parents in a dignified manner during their golden years, akin to how families cared for their elderly
prior to the industrial revolution. The risk was shifted from the old
retiree to the young worker and was backed by a solid counterparty,
the government. Ergo, this was a pension.

Before we go any further, it's worth noting that you might
already have access to a minimal amount of true pension income
at retirement. However, in all of our focus areas, these old-age,
government-provided mandatory workplace or Social Security pensions are typically expected to replace less than 50 percent of the
median earned income in retirement—meaning they will not, on
their own, provide an adequate source of lifetime income once you
reach the entitlement age (which, by the way, is steadily moving to
older ages). Instead, median earners can expect to replace from 32.6
percent (in the United Kingdom) to 52.3 percent (in Australia) from
these pensions. (The replacement rates for median-income earners
in the remaining countries are as follows: 38.3 percent in the United
States, 39.2 percent in Canada, and 40.6 percent in New Zealand
—see the Notes section for detailed sources.)

However, these income sources have built-in guarantees and
risk shifting, which are the hallmarks of true pensions. Despite the
rather modest payments they provide, they are guaranteed for your
lifetime. These are pensions in the true insurance, financial, and
economic senses of the word. There is counterparty to the contract,
the state government, standing behind the guarantee.

Okay, so what does all of this mean for you? Here's the main message of this chapter: while ordinary retirees and our politicians continue to debate the merits of private versus public provision of pensions, let's make sure you understand exactly what a pension really is. No more mixing up DB and DC pensions, and no more assuming DC pensioners are in the same boat as their DB counterparts. If you have a DC pension, you don't have the kind of smooth ride ahead that your DB peers can expect in retirement—unless you pensionize (part of) your nest egg. Finally, if you think your retirement income is safe because you have a job with a pension plan, you may want to check not only the type of plan you are in and what your income replacement rate will be in retirement (60 percent of your working income? 70 percent? 80 percent?), but also consider whether you're comfortable sharing the risk for your income stream in retirement with your employer over the 25, 30, or even 40 years after you leave the building.

With all that said, the rest of this book is built on three core beliefs:

1. The decline in pensions is real. And not only is it real—it's likely to speed up. No new pensions are coming, existing pensions are disappearing, and it's time for you to recognize and act from this new reality. You need to do something now to prepare for the years ahead, and that is to take responsibility for your own retirement income planning instead of waiting for politicians to bring back 1950s-style pensions.

2. True pensions provide the guarantees and certainty retirees require. A true pension starts at some advanced age and guarantees predictable income that matches the increasing cost of living for retirees. These kinds of pensions are rare and expensive. Don't underestimate the value of true

pensions and the protection they provide, especially if you do not belong to a DB pension plan (and even if you haven't got a clue how pension plans work). As the life-cycle model shows, a true pension is worth its weight in gold.

3. Finally, much ink has been spilled about ways to fix the problems in the current retirement income landscape across the United States, United Kingdom, Canada, Australia, and New Zealand—but you don't have to wait for change or leave it in anyone else's hands. This book provides you with all the essential tools you need to create your own pension plan for a secure retirement.

2

Planning for Longevity
Risks While Waiting for Your Return

Retirement planning, as practiced by most financial advisers and planners around the world, usually begins with a discussion of your money, investments, and retirement accounts. Now, while the question of how much to save for retirement is very important, we believe the process of retirement income planning should actually begin at the very end—the end of life, that is.

Accordingly, the best place to start planning for retirement income is the obituary section of the *Daily Telegraph* (in the United Kingdom), the *Wall Street Journal* (in the United States), the *Globe and Mail* (in Canada), or *The Australian* or New Zealand *Herald*. Yes, this may sound like a gloomy way to begin thinking about what's supposed to be the most rewarding period of your life, but hold on for a few minutes—you'll see the point soon.

Gather these one or two pages from the newspaper—the section does seem to grow over time, doesn't it?—and collect them for a few days, or even a few weeks. Sit yourself down with a blank piece of paper, a cup of coffee, and a pen. Now, look over each one of the lives chronicled in the obituaries and note the exact age at which these people died. Okay, spend some time reading about their lives and loved ones, but make sure to circle each age of death. Notice how some people lived to a glorious old age of 95, or perhaps even 100, while others barely made it to 70. In some very sad cases, you will see ages in the 40s and 50s, and perhaps even 20s and 30s, but those are rare. Most people live well into their so-called retirement years. Circle these numbers and keep track of them.

Next, create a table showing the number of years that each one of these people lived beyond the age of 65, which is a proxy for the numbers of years they spent in the retirement stage of life. Don't write down the negative numbers for the unfortunate few who didn't make it to 65; stay focused on the positive. Subtract 65 from the age at death and write down the resulting number on your pad of paper. So, if somebody passed away at 85, write down the number 20 (= 85 – 65). If they lived to 97, write down the number 32; if they lived to 66, write down the number 1; and if they died on their 65th birthday (now, what are the odds of that?), write down the number 0. Hopefully, you get the point and can create a long list of retirement longevity numbers like this: 27, 23, 14, 2, 7 . . . Bingo!

All joking aside, if you collect these numbers for a few days or weeks, your table should look something like Exhibit 2.1. This is a larger and more precise collection—notice the decimal points for fractions of years—recently created by a researcher at The QWeMA Group. There are 50 numbers in the table, showing 50 people who passed away in the United States over a few weeks in late 2014 and early 2015.

Hidden in those numbers were some interesting lives lived: a famous actress, a well-known writer, and even a few politicians and sports legends. We decided not to include the names for the sake of anonymity, but look carefully at the table. Notice how some people

Exhibit 2.1 Read the Obituaries: How Many Years Did They Spend in Retirement (Above the Age of 65)?

20.8	2.3	12.1	9	34.2
4.3	20.1	30.3	27.5	23.4
20.7	4.7	11.4	20.4	35.6
4.9	20.3	30.2	30.2	33.9
34.5	29.1	19.6	20.9	28.8
18.8	24.3	18.7	19.9	28.3
21	30.2	40.5	34.2	17
10.3	6.2	4.2	24	17.5
8.5	36.3	24.7	11.8	0.3
26.3	5.9	26.2	19.2	14.4

spent just a few years in the retirement stage of life, while others spent decades. You can see that three people lived to at least 100, and one (female) made it all the way to almost 106 (= 65 + 40.5). Spend some time to appreciate the variation or dispersion in those numbers, and ponder the question: Do you think they knew how long they would be spending in the retirement phase of life? And how long did they spend, on average?

If you calculate the arithmetic average of years in retirement— that is to say, you add them all up and divide by 50—you will get the number 19.7. Thus, the average amount of time these people spent in the so-called retirement stage of life was approximately 20 years. Yet some people spent almost 40 years in retirement and some barely made it for a few months—the variation is quite large!

Statisticians have a long-standing way of measuring this variation: they call it the "standard deviation," which measures the spread or dispersion of a set of data around the mean (average) value. The standard deviation for our set of numbers is 11. This means that most (66 percent) of the longevity numbers fall between 19 years plus 11 years, which is 30 years, and 19 years minus 11 years, which is 8 years.

If this is getting more technical than you care for, Exhibits 2.2 and 2.3 provide graphical representations of retirement longevity, together with a picture of the standard deviation just computed. Exhibit 2.2 shows the remaining lifetime for a U.S. male at age 65, while Exhibit 2.3 shows the mean and standard deviations for remaining years of life past age 65 for all regions. These exhibits tell you all you need to know about time spent in retirement. In Exhibit 2.2, you can see that the number of years spent in retirement roughly follows a kind of bell-shaped curve, like so many other things in life. More importantly, as you can see, the number of years you spend in retirement is random!

Exhibit 2.2 Remaining Lifetime for a 65-Year-Old (United States)

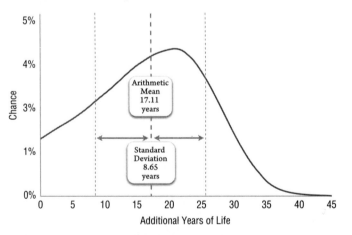

Source: Computations by The QWeMA Group at CANNEX based on United States Life Tables, 2009. See Notes for detailed source information.

Exhibit 2.3 Remaining Lifetime for a 65-Year-Old (All Areas)

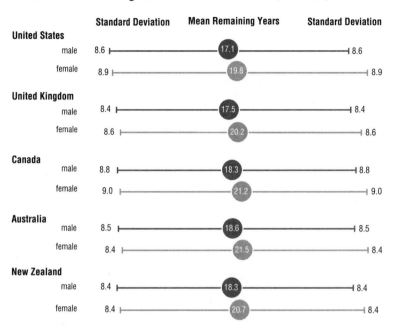

Source: Computations by The QWeMA Group at CANNEX based on country life tables. See Notes for detailed source information.

Here's the takeaway from all this discussion of variations and standard deviations: you don't really know how long you might live and thus how much you'll need to save for retirement. You might live as long as 40 years (at the right-hand side of the curve) or, sadly, it might be as short as 2 years (at the left-hand side of the curve). This variability is comparable to the risk or volatility of the stock market, but you probably understand and (with proper asset allocation) control your exposure to stock market risk.

The Grim Reaper's Coin Toss

In fact, one way to think of your chances of differing retirement years is like a Grim Reaper coin toss. If your toss comes out tails, your number will fall to the left of (below) the average, and if it comes out heads, it will fall to the right of (above) the average. We can't overemphasize how random this period can be, and that's just looking at existing data. In the future, medical breakthroughs, scientific achievements, and many other unknown factors can only increase this uncertainty.

How so? Just as one example, recent research seems to indicate that the Mediterranean diet, which is high in vegetables, fruits, whole grains, and olive oil, is associated with longer telomeres, the protective structures at the end of chromosomes, and this length correlates with longevity. So, according to this research, if we can get everyone to eat a Mediterranean-style diet, then the entire curve in Exhibit 2.2 will shift to the right, and the average amount of time spent by everyone in retirement will increase. That assumes, however, that some other factor to which we have widespread exposure doesn't decrease our longevity at the same time. Who knows with these things? So here is the bottom line once again: your longevity is just as uncertain as the gyrations and fluctuations of stock markets. Even if you think you can predict your longevity based on your family history, your health status and habits, or your gender—the truth is, you'd be making a very risky bet.

Introducing Longevity Risk

Pension experts—also known as insurance actuaries—call the concept underlying Exhibits 2.1, 2.2, and 2.3 longevity risk. This concept is at the core of many of the products you will read about in the next few chapters of this book. "Longevity risk" describes the risk that results from the fact that the precise length of time you will spend in retirement (and thus how many years of income you need to provide for yourself) is unknown. And here's the kicker—unlike the stock market, where taking on some risk is related to higher expected returns—longevity risk is entirely uncompensated. There's no (financial) payoff from a long life!

Another way to think about or represent longevity risk is by using a "probability distribution." Exhibit 2.4 gives you exactly that. These numbers were collected by researchers at statistics agencies in the United States, United Kingdom, Canada, Australia, and New Zealand—and they are based on millions of obituaries over thousands of days, so this is a lot more scientific than the little experiment you (and we) ran with our coffee and newspapers. These researchers also took population trends into account and made a number of other projections as well. The statistics underlying this kind of table are beyond the scope of this book, but the takeaway is of relevance just the same. Notice that the probability of living to any given age in the next couple of decades after retirement is high.

You can see from our table that the probability that a 65-year-old female will survive to age 100 ranges from 2 to 4 percent, while the

Exhibit 2.4 Conditional Probability of Survival at Age 65

	To Age	Male	Female	At Least One Member of a Couple
United States	70	89.88%	93.56%	99.35%
	80	57.58%	69.03%	86.86%
	90	18.31%	28.85%	41.87%
	100	0.96%	2.36%	3.30%
United Kingdom	70	91.14%	94.44%	99.51%
	80	60.05%	71.25%	88.51%
	90	18.54%	29.29%	42.40%
	100	0.68%	1.78%	2.44%

Exhibit 2.4 *(Continued)*

Canada	**70**	91.42%	94.86%	99.56%
	80	62.43%	73.95%	90.21%
	90	22.87%	35.14%	49.97%
	100	1.62%	3.80%	5.37%
Australia	**70**	92.59%	95.95%	99.70%
	80	64.62%	76.78%	91.79%
	90	22.36%	35.03%	49.56%
	100	0.98%	2.21%	3.16%
New Zealand	**70**	92.52%	95.35%	99.65%
	80	64.08%	74.26%	90.75%
	90	21.32%	31.67%	46.24%
	100	0.79%	1.73%	2.51%

Source: Computations by The QWeMA Group at CANNEX based on country life tables. See Notes for life table sources.

probability that a 65-year-old male will live to 100 is from under 1 to 2 percent. (Keep in mind that these numbers are for the entire population, not two particular people.)

Here is yet another important lesson about longevity (and its risk)—it is measurably higher for females than it is for males. In fact, if you paid attention while reading the obituary section, you would have noticed that although some females passed away at a relatively young age and some males passed away at a relatively old age, on average the retired females lived longer than the retired males. What this means from a practical point of view is that women must plan for a longer retirement.

Predicting Future Longevity

Some readers might wonder how (and where) exactly the numbers in all these exhibits come from and whether you can rely on them in making predictions or planning for the future. After all, it's one thing to display the age at which people died in the past, but how can you know the age at which people will die in the future? This question is a good one, but in the absence of any evidence to the contrary, the statisticians are assuming that history will repeat itself. If the obituaries over the past few years result in exhibits similar to 2.1 to 2.4, the assumption is that obituaries in 20, 30, or more years from now—including yours!—will exhibit the same pattern. Sure, there might be some improvements for the average, and you might get lucky, but the variation will always be there.

Take a look at Exhibit 2.4 again. There is a third column that shows the probability that at least one member of a couple will survive over a given period. Notice that the odds of one person in a couple living to a given age are larger than the odds of an individual living for the same time period. The probability that at least one member of the couple is alive can be computed by subtracting the number 1 from the product of the probabilities that either one is dead.

The implication is that if you are one member of a couple, the chance that one of you will live to age 90 or 100 (or any other age in the spectrum) is greater than your individual chance of living to that age. So if you are part of a couple and your nest egg must cover both you and your spouse, you need to take this joint probability into account in your planning, rather than relying on your individual probability of survival over time.

Finally, here is yet another important detail from Exhibit 2.4. Notice how the numbers in all three columns start off close to 100 percent and get closer to zero with age. This declining pattern can be plotted in a graph, which is what you see in Exhibit 2.5.

Exhibit 2.5 is often called a *survival probability curve*, and it provides a quick visual illustration of the fact that the odds of living longer decline exponentially with time and age. Very few people currently aged 65 will make it to 105 and few of them will die before age 75. The information conveyed in Exhibit 2.5 is exactly the same as the information displayed in Exhibit 2.4 (for the "United States" column, which we have used here to illustrate our point).

Remember, if you aren't alive, you are dead—so the two probabilities (the probability of survival and the probability of death) add up to 100 percent. The math can't get any easier than that!

How Should You Insure against Longevity Risk?

What we saw in the previous section is that the human life span is random. This insight makes retirement planning more difficult because we don't know with certainty—or in advance—when any of us will die and, thus, how long our money needs to last. As we've said, the risk we face of mismatching our finite financial resources to our life span is known as longevity risk.

Exhibit 2.5 Survival Probabilities for Men and Women—Age 65 (United States)

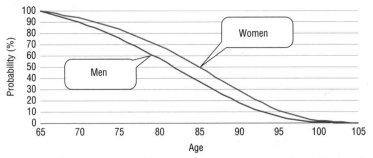

Source: Computations by The QWeMA Group at CANNEX based on United States Life Tables, 2009. See Notes for detailed source information.

Now that you have a basic understanding of longevity risk—what it is and why it's relevant—you are ready to perform some simple retirement income arithmetic. Later chapters will do the math in greater depth and with more accuracy, but for now we'll keep things simple. Imagine you are approaching your 60s and thinking seriously about retiring in the next few years. How much money do you need in your nest egg to finance your retirement?

Assume for the moment that you want an income or cash flow of exactly $50,000 per year to maintain your desired lifestyle. (This, too, will be addressed more carefully in later chapters to account for income taxes, inflation, and more. Again, we'll keep it simple for now.)

Continuing with our example, if you end up living in retirement for 40 years, you need approximately $50,000 times 40, which is $2 million, in your nest egg (ignoring interest, investment gains, the time value of money, and so on). But if you only end up living five years in retirement—and you saw some of these examples back in Exhibit 2.1—then you only need $50,000 times 5, which is $250,000, in your retirement account. As you can see, the difference between millions and hundreds of thousands—both legitimate estimates of what you might need—is enormous. And yet here's the catch: you don't know until after the fact if you need the big number or the small number.

If only you could read your obituary's date before you start retirement, financial life would be so much easier to plan for. (Now there's a thought!)

Will You Get Heads . . . or Tails?

But this uncertainty is precisely why longevity risk is more than just a morbid actuarial curiosity. It has real financial implications. Think about this: you spend your entire working life diligently saving every extra dollar or pound, diversifying, carefully allocating your assets, investing the maximum in your retirement savings accounts, all so you can retire with a million-dollar nest egg. But then, after a few years of retirement living, the bulk of the nest egg goes to somebody else because you got tails on the longevity risk coin toss. Sure, bequeathing all that money to your loved ones might not be such a bad thing—but is that why you were frugal for 30 working years?

Consider the other end of the spectrum: you might have built up a medium-sized nest egg, planning for an average retirement of about 25 years, only to get heads on the longevity coin toss and live 30, 35, or even more years after age 65. This outcome means that you will either have to reduce your standard of living or perhaps even borrow from your kids or against your assets. In either case, this is a very inefficient way to manage this stage of your life; it's like planning for a dinner party without having any idea how many guests will show up.

Get the point? Is this really a risk you want to take? Remember: DB pensions protect against this risk.

Now, one of the main concepts underlying this book is that many retirees are exposing themselves to longevity risk and probably don't know it yet. We believe that this is a risk that can be avoided, or at least managed properly, by pensionizing your nest egg—that is, taking some of your financial assets and converting them to a pension that pays a guaranteed income for the rest of your life. Pensionizing will protect you against the uncertainty about the length of your life and against numerous other risks you might face and may not even know about.

Curious? Read on.

3

How the Sequence of Returns Can Ruin Your Retirement

We know that in the back of your mind you might be wondering, "But isn't a solid portfolio of stocks and bonds good enough to finance my retirement?" After all, the investment industry has been preaching that, over the long term, there is no better place for your money than its mutual funds. This question brings us to the topics of downside protection and the curse of the sequence of returns. And no, this curse isn't some ancient medieval wizardry.

For many years members of the financial services industry— egged on by the media and even academics (but we're not naming names)—have preached the virtues of stocks, equity, and the buy-and-hold theory of investing. No doubt you have seen mountain-like charts of what a mere $1 or £1 invested back in the 1880s would have grown to by the year 2014. You might have also heard that the compound rate of return (or growth rate) from a diversified portfolio of stocks has been around 7 percent, after inflation, during the past century or so. This is true. We don't dispute any of it. But it also might be irrelevant when it comes to retirement income planning, and here is why.

How Long Will the Money Last?

Perhaps you are approaching retirement and you have a lump-sum nest egg valued at half a million dollars, or a million dollars, or more. No matter what T-bills and markets have done up until now, you are looking forward, not backward, and you are ready to turn your retirement savings account into income for life. But (despite what you read earlier in the chapter) let's say you are not ready to think about buying a personal pension. Instead, you want to create a retirement income plan using what the financial services industry calls a systematic withdrawal plan, or SWP—which enables you to sell a varying number of investment units to provide a constant monthly income (think dollar-cost averaging in reverse).

WHAT IS A SYSTEMATIC WITHDRAWAL PLAN?

A systematic withdrawal plan (SWP) is a combination of an investment asset allocation portfolio and a plan to withdraw a fixed dollar amount of money from the portfolio over time, without any regard for whether the portfolio and investments are doing well (up) or not (down).

A fundamental characteristic of a SWP is that the assets in this portion of your portfolio offer no guarantees, no downside protection, and no protection from longevity risk.

A SWP can also be thought of like the opposite of a dollar-cost-averaging (DCA) plan in which a fixed amount of money is used to automatically and periodically purchase stocks or mutual fund units regardless of price. The SWP is like a DCA in reverse. Although it isn't a product per se, it is meant to achieve the same thing as a pension, that is, provide a monthly stream of income—at least until the account runs out of money.

The first question you may be asking yourself is, "How long will my money last?" Let's answer this question using a simple example assuming a retirement savings nest egg of $100,000. (Remember, the example we're about to show works for nest eggs of any size, in addition to any units of currency.)

The basic laws of arithmetic tell us with unwavering accuracy exactly how long a nest egg will last when you make fixed withdrawals (that is, if you withdraw the same amount consistently) and generate known returns (that is, if your investment return does not fluctuate).

For example, if your current $100,000 portfolio is subjected to monthly withdrawals of $750 (which is $9,000 annually) and is earning a nominal rate of 7 percent per year (or 0.5833 percent per month), your nest egg will be completely empty during month 259. (A "nominal" rate of return is calculated before as expenses such as taxes, investment fees, and inflation are factored in.) Start this (doomed) process at age 65 and you will become ruined (that is, run out of money) halfway through age 86. Exhibit 3.1 illustrates the smooth and predictable path your portfolio will take on its way to ruin.

In this scenario, we know the inevitable date on which you will run out of money with absolute certainty, as the finance textbooks teach us that the present value of $750 for 260 periods under a periodic rate of 0.583 percent is exactly $100,000. Ergo, your $100,000 will only last until age 86.5. So if you plan to live to exactly age 86.5,

Exhibit 3.1 Portfolio Ruin with Constant Withdrawals and Constant Returns

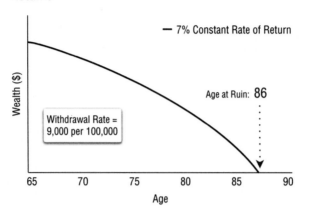

you should be fine. (By the way, this example holds with a portfolio of $200,000 and withdrawals of $18,000 per year, with a portfolio of $300,000 and withdrawals of $27,000 per year, and so on.)

Of course, if you plan to withdraw a lower $625 per month (which is $7,500 per year), the money runs out by month 466, and the nest egg lasts beyond the age of 100 for the same 65-year-old retiree. (The present value of $625 paid over 465.59 periods under a periodic rate of 0.5833 percent is also $100,000.)

So, if you knew *for sure* when you'd die and you knew *for sure* what your investments would earn over your lifetime, you could design a great retirement income plan.

But what happens if you (the hypothetical 65-year-old retiree) do not earn a constant 7 percent each and every year, but instead earn an arithmetic average of 7 percent over your retirement? How long does the money last, how variable is the final outcome, and what does that final outcome depend on?

Remember, investment returns fluctuate in this scenario (and in real life)—and you cannot rely on getting 7 percent every single year, even if you do earn it on average. For example, the U.S. stock market,

Exhibit 3.2 Illustrating an Arithmetic 7 Percent Average Return

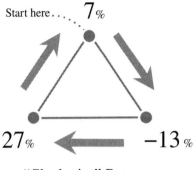

Start here.... $7_\%$

$27_\%$ ⬅ $-13_\%$

"Clockwise" Return

as proxied by the Standard & Poor's (S&P) 500, earned –38.47 percent in the year 2008, 23.49 percent in the year 2009, 12.64 percent in the year 2010, zero percent in the year 2011, 13.29 percent in the year 2012, 29.60 percent in the year 2013, and 11.39 percent in the year 2014. The arithmetic average of those seven years was 7.42 percent—but that was a far cry from what happened in any given year.

Now, since there are so many ways to generate an average return of 7 percent, let's give some structure to our problem. Imagine that the annual investment returns are generated in a cyclical and systematic manner. Exhibit 3.2 illustrates how it would work with a simple triangle—each point of the triangle represents a different year and a different investment return.

Clockwise Investment Returns

You can see from our exhibit that during the first year of retirement the portfolio earns 7 percent. In the second year of retirement it earns –13 percent, and in the third year of retirement it earns 27 percent. The arithmetic average of these numbers is exactly 7 percent, and each month we plan on withdrawing the same $750 as in the earlier case. In the fourth year we start the cycle again, and this cyclical process continues in three-year increments until the nest egg is exhausted and the money is gone. So here's the million-dollar question:

Do you think you will run out of money earlier or later than in the prior case, where returns were a smooth 7 percent each and every year?

If you think the answer is earlier, you are right. Indeed, since you started retirement on the wrong foot, generating a negative return (–13 percent) before the strongly positive return (+27 percent), you will run out of money a full three years earlier, at age 83. The 27 percent return in your third, sixth, and ninth (and so on) years of retirement isn't enough to offset the –13 percent returns in the second, fifth, and eighth (and so on) years of retirement. (This is akin to a 20 percent bull market in one year failing to undo the damage wrought by the 20 percent bear market in the previous year—or to needing a gain of 100 percent to make up for a loss of 50 percent.)

Note that the results in the cyclical returns scenario can be computed with just as much accuracy as they can in the constant return scenario, although you can't use a simple formula for the ruin time in this case. Instead, you must do this manually (what we like to call the "brute force" method).

Here's how to calculate the ruin time in this case:

- Take out a piece of paper and calculator. Start with $100,000 and force it to earn 0.5833 percent in the first month.

- Then withdraw $750 and have the remaining sum earn 0.5833 percent for the next month by multiplying $100,000 by 1.005833—or (0.007 / 12 + 1) by 100,000.

- Do this for 12 months, and then repeat for 12 months under an investment return of –1.0833 percent per month, which is a nominal –13 percent per year.

Exhibit 3.3 Portfolio Ruin with a "Clockwise" Sequence of Returns

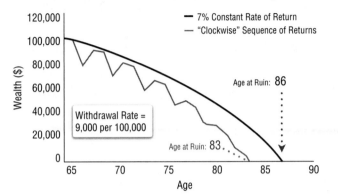

- Next, repeat for a further 12 months using an investment return of 2.2500 percent per month, which is a nominal 27 percent per year.

You can see that every 36 months the pattern repeats itself: start with twelve 0.5833 percent numbers, then twelve –1.0833 percent numbers, and finally twelve 2.2500 percent numbers. You should have a very long column of returns that, when charted, mimics the picture in Exhibit 3.3, with the account ultimately reaching zero shortly after your 83rd birthday. In this case—when the returns are "clockwise"—an average of 7 percent is worse than a smooth return of 7 percent every year.

Counterclockwise Returns

Now, what happens if you reverse the triangle and instead start in the other direction? In other words, what happens if you earn 7 percent, then 27 percent, and then –13 percent over and over again? Exhibit 3.4 displays the same triangle, but with the arrows going in the other direction.

Remember, the arithmetic average investment return is the same 7 percent regardless what side of the triangle is up when you

Exhibit 3.4 Reversing the Sequence of Returns

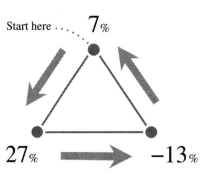

Start here · · · · $7_\%$

$27_\%$ ⟶ $-13_\%$

"Counterclockwise" Return

start retirement earnings and withdrawals. However, this time around the money runs out at age 89.5, as opposed to at ages 86.5 (with constant returns) and 83.33 (with clockwise returns). So, in this case, getting the highest returns before the negative return is better than getting 7 percent every year—it gives you more money than earning a constant 7 percent return would. Exhibit 3.5 shows this graphically.

Exhibit 3.5 Portfolio Ruin with a "Counterclockwise" Sequence of Returns

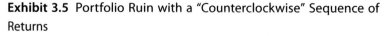

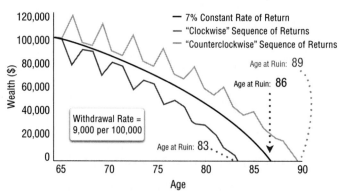

Exhibit 3.6 What Stop Did You Get on the Retirement Merry-Go-Round? The Impact of the Sequence of Returns on Portfolio Longevity

Return Sequence	Ruin Age	+/– Months
+7%, +7%, +7% ...	86.5	—
+7%, *–13%*, +27% ...	83.3	–38
+7%, +27%, *–13%* ...	89.5	36
–13%, +7%, +27% ...	81.1	–65
+27%, +7%, *–13%* ...	94.9	101

Before we move on, it's worth noting that this variance in outcomes would be even greater if we started with a particularly large number, such as –13 percent or 27 percent, as opposed to the 7 percent return we used as the starting year's return in all cases. For example, if the sequence were –13 percent, 7 percent, and then 27 percent, the age at which you would run out of money would be 81—the youngest yet. And if you started with 27 percent, not 7 percent, you'd run out of money at 94.92 years—the highest of all possible scenarios we examined.

Finally, Exhibit 3.6 summarizes the impact of all these various sequences on the "ruin age" (the age at which you run out of money), as well as the variation in months between the given sequence and the baseline case of a constant 7 percent return. You can see that this sequencing gap can get quite large—there is a 14-year gap between the lowest and highest ruin ages.

Triangles, Bulls, and Bears: The Retirement Income Circus

To be sure, the market doesn't move in perfect triangles. It is generally believed that stock markets, interest rates, and investment returns move in periodic cycles. These cycles—which also contain substantial "noise," or price and volume fluctuations that are random and meaningless—only become evident with hindsight, and are hence very difficult to predict or measure in advance. Nevertheless, these cycles can have a profound impact on the sustainability of your retirement income.

The bottom line is that if you retire and start to withdraw money from a diversified investment portfolio just as the market moves into a bear cycle, when markets are down, then your portfolio's longevity can be at risk.

This relatively obvious observation is often called the "sequence-of-returns risk." You are most at risk from a negative sequence of returns during the so-called "retirement risk zone"—the years immediately preceding and following retirement, when you have the largest amount of money at stake, the fewest number of years left in the workforce, and thus the smallest capacity to recover from market downturns.

Can Buckets Bail Out a Poor Sequence of Returns?

Now, despite everything we've just said, you may be thinking, "I can protect myself from a poor sequence of returns by putting an amount equivalent to a few years of my income needs into safe investments. Then if the rest of my investments go down, I just won't touch them until the markets recover." This is often called the "bucketing" strategy—where income needs for the first few years of retirement are segregated from the rest of the investment portfolio and placed in safe "buckets." This strategy is popular with many people because it aligns with how they often save—putting all of their spare coins in a (metaphorical) jar that will eventually provide enough to buy a special item. But retirement is different, because no one knows which years the "safe" bucket should be replenished. So although this strategy gives the illusion of safety, in actuality it exposes your nest egg to more risk.

Think about it this way. If you start with an allocation of 50 percent cash and 50 percent equities and plan to draw from the cash bucket to meet your income needs in the first few years of retirement, then as you draw down the cash bucket, your total asset allocation will drift more and more toward equities. Adopting the bucketing approach to retirement income planning will affect your total asset allocation, and the implicit exposure to equities will fluctuate over time (as your overall allocation to equities and their higher volatility increases as you empty your cash bucket). Then, if you experience a poor initial sequence of investment returns—so that you have been forced to liquidate all of your cash investment—you might find yourself with 100 percent equity exposure well into retirement, and possibly deep into a bear market. You will have traded *income stability* for *asset instability*. Don't let optical illusions fool you into thinking your retirement income portfolio is safer than it really is.

So how can you protect yourself against sequence-of-returns risk? As we have touched on, and will continue to explain in this book, pensionization—converting a fraction of your retirement savings to guaranteed lifetime income—allows you to get more from less with your retirement savings. We will discuss exactly how to do that in Part Two—but before we do, there's one more risk we need to explore in the next chapter.

4

Inflation
The Great Money Illusion

By now, you may be wondering when we are going to provide detailed examples of how to pensionize your nest egg and allocate your retirement accounts across the various retirement income products available. But before we are ready to do that, we need to have a conversation about a very fundamental aspect of money itself—inflation. In this chapter, we're going to explore how to ensure that your nest egg doesn't rot away in the nest before you spend it.

You've undoubtedly heard the expression "a bird in the hand is worth two in the bush." While this saying probably isn't about inflation, it certainly fits because a dollar today is worth more than a dollar tomorrow, and both are worth much more than a dollar will be in 20 years. Now, why is this? Because that same dollar you started out with will buy much less over time. Sure, this loss of purchasing power might not be evident on the time scales of weeks, months, or even years, but it definitely becomes evident over decades and over the term of your retirement—possibly 30 or 40 years.

Here's an example. Perhaps you remember what a stamp, a dozen eggs, or a quart of milk cost 20 or 30 years ago. It was a fraction of

Exhibit 4.1 How a Dollar Decays over Time

	United States	United Kingdom	Canada	Australia	New Zealand
	Inflation Rate (%)	Inflation Rate (%)	Inflation Rate (%)	Inflation Rate (%)	Inflation Rate (%)
1965	1.7	4.5	2.5	4.0	3.4
1970	5.9	7.9	3.4	3.9	6.7
1975	9.1	24.9	10.8	15.1	14.5
1980	13.5	15.1	10.2	10.1	17.1
1985	3.6	5.7	4.0	6.7	15.4
1990	5.4	7.0	4.8	7.3	6.1
1995	2.8	2.7	2.2	4.6	3.8
2000	3.4	0.8	2.7	4.5	3.0
2005	3.4	2.0	2.2	2.7	3.0
2010	1.6	3.3	1.8	2.8	2.3
2013	1.5	2.6	0.9	2.4	1.3
	3.9	5.4	3.9	4.9	5.7

Average geometric inflation rate, 1965–2013

Note: Data for the United Kingdom for the period 1965–1988 is the Retail Price Index (RPI), not the Consumer Price Index. In the period 1965–1988 the U.K. government used RPI as the official inflation indicator. RPI data for the period 1965–1988 was obtained from "Annual Abstract of Statistics", 2001 edition. Office for National Statistics. www.ons.gov.uk (accessed January 15, 2015).

Source: "Inflation, consumer price (annual %)". The World Bank, International Monetary Fund, Inflation and Financial Statistics and data files. http://data.worldbank.org/indicator/FP.CPI.TOTL.ZG/countries/ (accessed January 15, 2015).

today's cost, which is essentially all to be blamed on the impact of inflation: it causes money to decay over time, like rotten fish and spoiled eggs. (Okay, we are pushing it.)

Exhibit 4.1 displays the annual inflation rate in the United States, the United Kingdom, Canada, Australia, and New Zealand during the past 50 years, in five-year increments. The first column shows the year in question, and the remaining columns show the inflation rate in that year—as measured by the change in the consumer price index (CPI). In Exhibit 4.2, we illustrate the corrosive impact of inflation on a 1965 dollar or pound (more on this in a moment).

Inflation statistics are collected by government offices around the world and are also readily available on the websites of most financial institutions.

Exhibit 4.2 How Much Is My 1965 Dollar or Pound Worth?

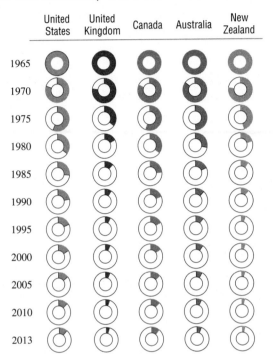

Note: Data for the United Kingdom for the period 1965–1988 is the Retail Price Index (RPI), not the Consumer Price Index. In the period 1965–1988 the U.K. government used RPI as the official inflation indicator. RPI data for the period 1965–1988 was obtained from "Annual Abstract of Statistics", 2001 edition. Office for National Statistics. www.ons.gov.uk (accessed January 15, 2015).

Source: "Inflation, consumer price (annual %)". The World Bank, International Monetary Fund, Inflation and Financial Statistics and data files. http://data.worldbank.org/indicator/FP.CPI.TOTL.ZG/countries/ (accessed January 15, 2015).

You can see from our table that in the year 1980 the inflation rate ranged from about 10 to 17 percent, compared to a range of about 5 to 7 percent 10 years later, and 1 to 5 percent in the year 2000. Notice how over just a few years the inflation rate can suddenly increase unexpectedly after periods of relative calm. You can also see how misleading an average rate is. For example, the geometric average inflation rate during the entire period (from 1965 to 2010) ranged from 3.9 to 5.7 percent, but you can see that over this period and in these regions, inflation had a low point of just less than 1 percent and a high point of almost 25 percent.

Exhibit 4.2 shows this decay process graphically. Had you started with $1 or £1 in the year 1965, it would have shrunk gradually with each passing year. Notice how over a period of 50 years the purchasing power declines by as much as 95 percent. Had you put $100, $1,000, or $10,000 dollars or pounds in a piggy bank for 50 years, your lump sum at the end might purchase less than 5 percent of what it could have bought when you first socked it away! Although we don't know exactly what the inflation rate will be going forward, there is no reason to believe this decaying process will end any time soon. Now, central banks often make promises that they will keep inflation moderate, but do you trust that the central banks can fulfill on this mission? Do you trust their definition of inflation? Most importantly, does that overall inflation number actually apply to you? More on this next.

What Does This Mean for Retirees?

When you are young, earnings (in the form of salary) tend to keep up with inflation. In all likelihood your wages grow at a positive real (after-inflation) rate over time—in other words, your salary increase is higher than inflation, so inflation is just not that much of a threat in your working years. And if inflation picks up, you will likely demand a raise, or perhaps a bonus, from your employer to keep up with the cost of living.

But in the area of retirement income planning, things are very different. The relatively low inflation rates we have seen over the past few years might actually be lulling us into a false sense of security. This is because low numbers can be easily ignored. Yet, over long time horizons the effects of inflation can be deadly to your financial life, especially if you are not compensated for inflation risk

Exhibit 4.3 Inflation: What Does a $1,000 Payment *Really* Buy You?

	Inflation Rate			
Year #	0%	1%	2%	4%
1	$1,000	$990	$980	$961
5	$1,000	$951	$905	$818
10	$1,000	$905	$819	$670
15	$1,000	$861	$741	$548
20	$1,000	$819	$670	$449
25	$1,000	$779	$606	$367
30	$1,000	$741	$549	$301
35	$1,000	$705	$496	$246

Note: Monthly compounding

and if you don't know your own inflation rate. Yes, one of the main financial risks we face as we age is our unknown and age-specific personal inflation rate.

Let's look at the issue of inflation in retirement income terms. Exhibit 4.3 illustrates the impact of even relatively benign inflation rates over long periods of time. Now, we don't know what inflation will be like in the future; this table just gives us some points of comparison.

Here's how to read this exhibit: Imagine you are getting a $1,000 pension income check every single month of your retirement years but that this check is not adjusted for inflation. What this means is that your nominal income stays at $1,000 (that is, the check is always made out for $1,000), but its real purchasing power declines steadily with time. So as you age, the same check buys you less. The table shows exactly how much $1,000 will buy you in today's dollars, depending on the annual rate of inflation going forward.

Notice that increasing the inflation rate from 2 percent to 4 percent per year will erode the purchasing power of your $1,000 by almost 40 percent at the 25-year horizon. (We picked 25 years as it is the median remaining life span for a newly retired couple, and a 2 percent to 4 percent inflation rate is arguably a reasonable summary range for inflation.)

So, imagine you bought 1,000 eggs in year one, with each egg costing a year 1 dollar. If the real price of eggs remains steady and you have average inflation of 2 percent, then by year 25, you could only buy 606 eggs (assuming inflation for eggs is 2 percent) with your $1,000. And if inflation hovers around 4 percent, you will be down to 367 eggs. Now, you may personally not care about eggs and would be happy to buy fewer of them over time, but the point is that this analogy applies to everything you consume, from gasoline to plane tickets to prescription medication to pet food.

The CPI-ME and the CPI-YOU

So far, we've only discussed generic inflation rates, but the inflation story gets even more interesting when you include personal inflation rates. In the United States, the Department of Labor has created an entirely new experimental inflation index for the elderly. They call it the CPI-E, and it is meant to better capture the inflation rate unique to Americans aged 62 and older.

You may be asking yourself why inflation would be different for the elderly. Indeed, how does inflation even get measured? The answer to these questions comes down to spending habits. Boiled down to its essence, statisticians measure inflation partially based on how we spend our money.

Here's how it works: inflation statisticians measure price changes for hundreds of categories and items each month. Some of these items increase in price while others decline or stay the same. The weights placed on the different categories and items in the CPI—that is, how much impact spending on a particular item and any change in that item's price has on the overall CPI—reflect our average spending habits. If the typical consumer spends three times as much money on banana products as on avocado products, then the index weight placed on bananas is three times as high as the index weight placed on avocados, regardless of your allergy to bananas and love for avocados.

The U.S. consumer price index for urban wage earners and clerical workers (CPI-W) reflects the spending habits of this group, which includes about 32 percent of the U.S. population (and is a continuation of the historical index that was introduced after World War I for use in wage negotiations). In looking at the CPI-W, we can see that working Americans spend about four times more on food and beverages than they do on apparel, and they spend eight times more on housing than they do on recreation, and so on. To make a long story short, in the United States, the relative importance placed on the various subcomponents of the consumer price index differs for the regular index (CPI-W) and the elderly index (CPI-E).

For example, medical care has twice the weight in the CPI-E as it does in the CPI-W, because the elderly spend a greater fraction of their income on medical care. Conversely, statisticians have discovered that Americans in their 40s and 50s spend almost three times more on food and alcohol than on medical care. But by the time they reach their late 70s, their food and alcohol expenditure is only a fraction of their medical care expenses. Unsurprisingly, other countries, such as the United Kingdom and Australia, have investigated whether retirees experience rates of inflation that differ from nonretired households, and have contemplated using a specific inflation rate for retired households.

Does the CPI Measure Your Spending?

Although the CPI-E is unique to the United States, the same issues apply anywhere in the world. The bottom line is that inflation indices assume a given representative consumer who may not represent you at all. Indeed, researchers have found that the generic CPI is not a good measure of price increases faced by individual households, and that a significant proportion of senior households experience inflation rates considerably higher than the CPI.

How can this be? As we said earlier, in recent years the overall inflation rate has been quite low. But even in this low-inflation environment, the costs of some goods and services have risen. Recent examples of goods and services whose price has risen faster than the official rate of inflation include medical care, gasoline and other transportation and travel-related costs, and many food items (including eggs!).

The lesson here is to be aware that the costs of both essential and nonessential activities may increase even as the general price increases are low.

The moral of our inflation story is that it is often higher for retirees. But our point here is not that you should add another percentage point to your retirement income inflation projections. The fact that some agencies bother to compute an inflation rate for retirees should remind us that inflation is personal. After all, if there is a CPI-E, why not a CPI-ME or a CPI-YOU? Depending on where you live, how you spend your money, how old you are, and even your gender, your personal inflation rate is different than the average. In fact, in the United Kingdom, the Office of National Statistics runs an official personal inflation calculator, intended to help users understand how their personal inflation rate is affected by what they spend their money on.

A Reality Check for Your Retirement Spending

The issue of inflation is absolutely critical for retirement income planning, and there are two (and only two) things you can do about the problem of inflation: think in real terms and invest in real products. Let us explain both of these carefully.

First, think in real terms. When you are estimating your needs, make sure to budget in a margin of decay for inflation. If you think you will need $5,000 a month to live on, make sure to increase that by 2 percent to 4 percent next year, and then another 2 percent to 4 percent the year after, and so on. (In fact, we will go over this specifically in Part Three, where we provide the seven steps to pensionize your own retirement income.)

The same issue applies to investment returns. If you are being promised a return of 5 percent, then make sure to subtract a few percentage points for inflation.

Second, invest in real products. In addition to thinking in real terms, you should also invest in products that try to keep up with the cost of living. Some investments are actually indexed to inflation and will pay interest, or dividends based on the CPI. With these products, the greater the inflation rate, the more you are paid. So, for example, if you are promised a real return of 4 percent and inflation is 3 percent, you will get a return of approximately 7 percent (think of real return bonds, inflation-linked annuities, and similar instruments). (Keep in mind that if you invest in real products, you have implemented the "think in real terms" part of our advice here.)

There are also some investment products that provide returns that are weakly linked to inflation but don't actually provide payouts in inflation-adjusted terms. These include a diversified portfolio of stocks. With overall inflation, stock returns might increase beyond inflation in the long run, but in the short run there might be substantial dispersion—that is, your returns may bounce around unpredictably and not track inflation at all.

In the end, you may want to use a mix of products to guard against the effects of inflation. You may choose to purchase indexed annuities, if they are available to you. However, this is only one way to protect against inflation risk—and keep in mind that your personal rate of inflation may be higher or lower than the indexed increases. Our main point is that you need to be aware of the reality of inflation, the difficulty of predicting inflation over the long term, and the ways in which you might protect yourself from its impact.

What Have We Learned So Far?

We've now reached the end of Part One. What have we learned so far? We reviewed the new risks that emerge from the shadows just as you think your journey to retirement is coming to an end: longevity risk, sequence-of-returns risk, and the threat of "decaying dollars" or inflation.

We also discussed, in general terms, ways you can protect yourself against those risks: by investing in products that transfer risk away from your personal balance sheet, and by thinking in real terms. But this advice, while helpful, is too piecemeal to be of much use. What people planning for retirement need is an integrated strategy that brings together the products available to protect against the new risks of retirement and that provides a way to effectively allocate your nest egg among them. This is exactly what we are going to provide in Part Two, which brings it all together—building a modern solution that is actually hundreds of years old.

TWO

**Developing a Sustainable Retirement
Solution: The Modern Approach That Is
Hundreds of Years Old**

5

Beyond Asset Allocation
Introducing Product Allocation

In Part One of this book, we reviewed the new risks you face as you approach retirement. Now that you can see those risks coming, how do you protect yourself against them?

In this part, we outline the new approach of product allocation, which will augment asset allocation to guide you through retirement; explore the true function of pensions; help you calculate your Retirement Sustainability Quotient; and ask the most difficult question you will ever have to answer about your retirement goals. Curious? Dive in!

Product Allocation: New Baskets for Your Nest Egg

So far, we have discussed the decline in pensions and the need for pensionized income. We've told you the new risks you face as you leave the accumulation stage of financial planning and begin to use your assets to fund your retirement. The main takeaway from the preceding section of the book is that asset allocation, despite its value in the accumulation stage of life, is not sufficient to protect you into and through retirement.

Now, you've already done a lot of work preparing for retirement. Today, if your financial adviser asked you, "How much would you like to allocate to stocks, and how much to bonds?" you'd probably have an answer. If she asked you, "How much would you like to allocate to domestic stocks, and how much to international equities?," you'd probably have some thoughts on that. And if you were asked, "Would you like to focus on value stocks (like Coca-Cola) or growth stocks (like Google)?," you'd probably have an opinion on that, too.

But what if your adviser asked you, "How much of your retirement nest egg would you like to allocate to annuities? At what age would you like to start to annuitize your wealth? How much pensionized income would you like in retirement—and what's your pension income gap?" Would you know how to answer these questions?

These are not asset allocation questions—they are product allocation questions.

What is "product allocation"? It is the process of allocating your financial resources to different kinds of financial and insurance products to protect you against the new risks you face as you transition into and through retirement. Different asset classes—stocks and bonds—have different risk and return characteristics and respond differently to the same economic conditions and cycles. Similarly, different product classes behave differently in the same conditions and protect your financial future from varying sources of risk.

Three Product Silos

Today, you can think about retirement income products as grouped into three silos:

- First, there are traditional mutual funds, exchange-traded funds, stock accounts, and other accumulation-focused accounts, which offer growth potential but no lifetime guarantees. Retirement income is generated from these accounts by periodically selling an appropriate number of units. These products are used to protect against inflation risk, with the hope and expectation that your funds will grow faster than inflation. They also preserve liquidity (you can generate income as you need it) and the hope of a financial legacy.

- Second, there are products that are designed to provide a lifetime income—including defined benefit (DB) occupational pension plans, public retirement income programs, and life annuity products purchased by individuals. These allocations protect against longevity risk, but they typically come at the cost of complete irreversibility and loss of liquidity. A life annuity purchase is a one-way street: once you've allocated funds to an annuity, you can't undo the decision. You could think of anything in this silo as a *lifetime payout income annuity*, whether you are purchasing these products before retirement (as a deferred income annuity), at retirement, or in retirement.

- Finally, there are financially engineered products that fall in between these two silos. These are the modern sequence-of-returns-protected investments, and among the most common are variable annuities with guaranteed living benefits (often known by the shorter "alphabet soup" acronym of VAs with GLBs), and fixed indexed annuities with guaranteed living benefits (or FIAs with GLBs). These products provide guaranteed income (like a life annuity from the second silo) as well as exposure to the stock market (like an account from the first silo). At the most basic level, a VA with GLB is like a mutual fund portfolio with a guaranteed payout each year, while an FIA with GLB is a contract that provides the contract owner with annual interest based on the performance of a stock market index. Products in this silo are a bit like hybrid cars, which run on both gasoline and electricity, switching as conditions require.

To be clear, these three silos are drawn from the existing universe of retirement income products. The world of retirement income planning is constantly evolving, and we expect new products to enter the retirement income space and new features to be added to existing products. In the next few chapters, we will look at each of these silos in turn to see how they can be used to provide income in retirement. But at a basic level, how are they different?

The Spectrum of Retirement Income Silos

Think of the three silos as three points on a spectrum. At one end of our retirement income product spectrum you can find lifetime payout annuities (or "life annuities") and DB pensions, which provide guaranteed lifelong income through all market conditions, are perhaps adjusted for inflation, and usually leaving nothing behind when the annuitant dies.

At the other end of the spectrum are nonguaranteed sources of income, such as stocks and mutual funds. These sources of retirement income are typically what people think of as making up their nest egg, and these investments are usually individually held and controlled. In this silo, you may have taxable, tax-deferred, or tax-free accounts holding mutual funds, unit trusts, exchange-traded funds, and individual shares, as well as bonds, term deposits, and more. These investments perform differently in different market conditions, and hence these assets are often carefully allocated across different classes to enhance returns and reduce volatility. But what unifies all the assets in this silo is that their account values are usually not guaranteed and will fluctuate over time.

In the middle of that spectrum is the newest arrival on the product horizon: products that fall between nonguaranteed investments and guaranteed investments, and include elements of both. These products typically pay a guaranteed monthly income for life (like a life annuity) in addition to maintaining some market exposure. Although there are several different (clunky) acronyms used to refer to these products, as noted earlier, we will focus on the variable annuity with guaranteed living income benefit in this silo.

Variable annuities with a GLB can be thought of like a pendulum that swings between silos 1 and 3, switching between providing annuitized income and investment growth—depending on market conditions and your income needs. The variable annuity plus GLB pendulum swings from side to side, behaving (one on hand) like an mutual fund and on the other like a life annuity, but never quite catching up to the performance of either. When stock markets are doing well and the VA plus GLB combination mimics the performance of a mutual fund, it will never quite catch up to the returns earned by the (nonprotected) fund because of the higher fees charged for the guarantee. They create a drag of almost 1 percent in performance that eats into your investment returns. Likewise, when markets are in a funk and stocks are down, the VA plus GLB behaves like an income annuity—but never quite generates the 8 percent, 9 percent, or even 10 percent for life that you might have earned from a lifetime payout annuity. Of course, the reason for the substandard performance relative to both products is precisely because of the benefit they provide: you get to swing from one to the other based on market conditions. In the language of financial professionals, you have been granted an option to select the best of both worlds—but at a price!

Now, each of those product categories provides benefits and trade-offs, and accordingly your funds can be allocated among them instead of relying on only one category. This will enable you to capture the upside potential while minimizing the downside risk.

How Do the Silos Stack Up?

One way to think about the different retirement income investment choices is to compare the extent to which they protect you from the new risks of retirement. These new risks include longevity (the risk of living longer than your money), inflation, and market or sequence of returns risk. How do the three silos protect against each of these risks?

You can see from Exhibit 5.1 that there is no one silo that protects against all risks and provides all benefits. As we've said, it intuitively makes sense to spread your nest egg resources across these three product silos—to capture the longevity insurance from life annuities, for example, as well as the growth potential from traditional mutual funds or unit funds.

We're going to examine the benefits and trade-offs in detail, but first we'll look more closely at life annuities, the oldest entrant in the retirement income field.

Exhibit 5.1 Three Product Silos: Their Benefits and How They Protect against Retirement Risk

Product Silo	Product Type	Protection against Retirement Risks			Benefits		
		Longevity	Inflation	Sequence of Returns	Legacy Value & Liquidity	Sustainability	Asset Growth Potential
Guaranteed Income for Life	Immediate Income Annuities	✓	if you purchase an annuity with a COLA adjustment	✓	✗	✓	✗
	Deferred Income Annuities	✓		✓	✗	✓	✗
Guaranteed Income + Growth Potential	Variable Annuities with GLB	✓	only if markets perform well	✓	yes—but less than a SWP account	✓	✓
	Fixed Indexed Annuities with GLB	✓		✓		✓	✓
Asset Growth Potential	SWP Account	✗	only if markets beat inflation	✗	✓	only if markets perform well	✓

6

An Introduction to Life Annuities

With any luck, our description of the new risks of retirement in the first part of the book didn't concern you too much and you are actually looking forward to the possibility of 35 years of retirement (or perhaps even longer!). Still, what should cause some apprehension is the chance that your retirement nest egg (your financial capital) will not last as long as you do. Paying for 30 to 40 years of retirement can create quite a burden on you, your portfolio, and perhaps even your children. The good news is that you can insure against this kind of risk, and at a very reasonable price.

Now, yes, one normally thinks about buying insurance to protect you if terrible things happen, like your house burning down, or your car getting totaled, or you being paralyzed from an accident, or some other horrible thing like that. But the truth is that these days you can also buy insurance against things that are only kind of bad, including almost anything that might cause you personal stress or economic discomfort. For example, you can buy insurance to protect you against the price of your morning coffee doubling next year as a result of a drought in the Ivory Coast, and you can buy insurance to protect your stock portfolio from suffering losses in the market, which can be catastrophic when you are about to retire.

In general, our view on insurance policies—whether they are extended warranties, product replacement plans, or life insurance—is that you should only pay to insure against financially devastating events that can wreak serious havoc on your personal finances. We believe you should not waste money on insurance policies and products that only protect you against financial losses that are relatively minor. (This will vary between individuals and depend on your total resources. If a kidney transplant for your beloved cat will bankrupt you, go ahead and purchase pet insurance from the veterinarian. Otherwise, save the cost of premiums instead.)

Back to our point: As we've demonstrated, longevity risk can potentially ruin your retirement if you don't have a true pension, and longevity insurance can protect you against longevity risk. At first consideration, we agree that it might seem quite odd to buy insurance against a blessing (living a long life), but the insurance doesn't protect you against living a long life—it protects you against the cost of this outcome if it materializes. Moreover, this longevity insurance is embedded inside a product that you are already familiar with by now—yes, pensions.

Pension Contributions as Insurance Premiums

Think about how a full and proper pension works. Once you retire, you become entitled to a monthly income that lasts for the rest of your natural life. This pension obviously isn't free to provide. Most likely your employer (if they offer such a pension) will have deducted something from your paycheck each and every month to fund it. You can think about these deductions as if they are insurance premiums paid to an insurance company while you are working. Then, when you retire, the periodic income a pension generates is your insurance payoff. This payoff usually continues to your spouse if he or she outlives you.

Let's do some basic annuity math to demonstrate how a pension might work (leaving aside inflation, taxes, and other real-world variables for the moment). In the simplest of cases, if you are receiving $1,000 per month from age 65 and you live to age 105, your pension will pay $480,000 over the course of your life (that is, $1,000 per month × 480 months). On the other hand, if you only survive to age 80, the total payout will be $180,000 (or $1,000 per month × 180 months). The basic rule of pension math is: the longer you live, the greater the payoff. Now, given that basic rule, we're suggesting you can think about pensions like your insurance against longevity risk.

As you can see from our discussion so far, a pension has characteristics similar to a bond that pays monthly interest (the pension check), in addition to its elements of insurance. Whether your pension behaves more like a bond or more like insurance depends entirely on how long you live. If you don't end up living very long, your pension may act like a bond in your portfolio, in that it simply repays your own money back to you at regular intervals. But if you live longer than expected, your pension will be more like an insurance policy, which not only returns your money but adds more (possibly much more). Just like with your house insurance, if the risk against which you are insuring is realized (you live longer than expected), you receive value from the insurance company that may well exceed the total value of the premiums you paid. This is exactly the protection that pensions provide.

Buying a Personal Pension

So where do you get your longevity insurance if you don't have a pension from your employer? The answer is that you can buy your own personal pension. It will likely not be called a pension, but a life annuity, and, as we've said, that is the term we will use in this book to describe a personal pension.

Now, you might think we are talking about some kind of life insurance—but we aren't. Life insurance (perhaps best understood as premature death insurance) pays off when you die. But the financial products we are thinking about pay off during your lifetime—if you don't die. And what distinguishes these products from any other kind of investment product are "mortality credits," or contributions that are reallocated from those who die to those who survive, and which form part of the payments to surviving purchasers.

Before we go any further, please note that we are not advocating you turn all of your cash over to an insurance company to purchase a life annuity. We will discuss how much of your nest egg to invest in annuities later, but we aren't quite there yet.

Back to annuities. An annuity is actually an ancient product, reaching back to Roman times. Life annuities were paid to Roman soldiers in exchange for their military service, and wealthy Romans could bequeath an income for life to their heirs. Today, anyone can give an insurance company a lump sum in exchange for monthly income for life—no military service or rich relatives required. You can buy a life annuity at retirement with one lump-sum payment (this is known as an "immediate annuity"), or you can buy annuities slowly, a few thousand dollars' worth at a time, starting at or before retirement (these are immediate annuities purchased over time). Finally, you can buy annuities at or before retirement and elect to start receiving payments later (this is a "deferred income annuity").

If you are interested in purchasing a life annuity, you can get quotes (different insurance companies will pay out at different rates) and compare your alternatives. You can also purchase many different riders (or options) that will affect the payout you will receive, including riders to provide inflation protection, cost of living increases, and guaranteed payout periods (i.e., you are guaranteed to receive payments for a set period, whether you are living or not). You can also buy term annuities (for a specified term, not a lifetime annuity), joint annuities that pay out as long as one member of a couple is alive, and so on. Individual annuities can be bought with funds from different kinds of investment accounts, and when you are buying a life annuity, you can typically choose between options that affect how the payments are taxed.

In sum, there's a lot to consider if you are contemplating purchasing a life annuity. But right now, we're just thinking and talking about annuities at a very basic level and in contrast to the other retirement income product silos. No need to worry about the specific annuity you might want yet.

When Should You Buy an Annuity?

Okay. If you think you'd like a self-purchased pension in retirement, when should you buy it? Recall that we said you can buy annuities right when you retire (or later) and start receiving payment immediately (an immediate income annuity), or you can buy annuities before retirement, even well before retirement, and start receiving payment at retirement or later (a deferred income annuity). Exhibit 6.1 shows some sample prices for immediate and deferred income annuities purchased at ages 35, 50, and 65, and with payouts starting at ages 65, 75, and 85.

You can see from this table that for $1,000 of monthly income you will pay vastly different amounts, depending on both your age at the time of purchase and your age at the time the payouts start. The most expensive choice from the nine listed in the table is to purchase an immediate annuity at age 65. Delaying either your purchase or your payouts to an older age reduces the cost considerably. And why is that? First, the same amount of yearly income, received over a shorter period of time, costs less. And second, as you age, more people born in the same year as you die, meaning the mortality credits increase over time.

Note that these numbers will change from day to day, depending on market conditions such as interest rates, and depending on the specific bells and whistles you might want added to your life annuity (such as a guarantee that your children will get some residual value, or perhaps that your spouse can continue the income when you die).

Exhibit 6.1 Lump–Sum Cost of Immediate and Deferred Annuity Payouts

Cost of $1,000 per month of annuity income starting at age ...			
Age at which you buy the annuity:	65	75	85
35	$56,015	$31,770	–
50	$94,890	$43,650	$16,425
65	$187,335	$82,100	$25,920

Source: CANNEX Financial Exchanges for, non-COLA-adjusted nonqualified annuity income for a U.S. male in California. Average of highest and lowest quotes on July 24, 2014.

To contrast with the information in Exhibit 6.1, we also collected the historical price of $1,000 of monthly income for life, starting at age 65, over the past 10 years.

Exhibit 6.2 shows us that the cost of the same amount of annuity income has changed over time. Why do you think this might be?

There are a number of reasons why prices for life annuities change because a variety of factors affect how annuities are priced. These factors include changes in interest rates and in the "yield curve" (which is a graph that illustrates the relationship between yield and maturity among similar fixed-income securities). Increases in longevity—how long people are living—also affect annuity prices. Over time, as longevity increases and fewer people die at any given age, the amount of money available to redistribute to survivors is reduced. "Adverse selection," or the phenomenon of healthier-than-average people buying annuities compared to the population as a whole, causes issuers to adjust annuity prices as they attempt to match the longevity of purchasers with the annuity products purchased. Finally, changes in competitiveness and competition in the insurance marketplace also influence how much a purchaser will pay for lifetime annuity

Exhibit 6.2 Cost of $1,000 in Monthly Lifetime Annuity Income, Starting at Age 65

Year	Male	Female
2004	$157,432	$167,818
2005	$157,255	$167,817
2006	$151,700	$161,363
2007	$151,524	$160,966
2008	$147,953	$155,843
2009	$156,500	$165,502
2010	$170,116	$178,410
2011	$174,828	$182,952
2012	$187,008	$195,216
2013	$183,728	$191,571
Average	$163,804	$172,746

Source: CANNEX Financial Exchanges for non-COLA-adjusted qualified annuity income with a 10-year guarantee for California. Average of highest and lowest quotes.

income. All of these factors influence how much an annuity will cost for people in the same position but buying at different times. And there's still more to the annuity payout story, in the form of mortality credits—which we'll get to shortly.

Annuities versus Term Deposits

Some readers might think that our description of a life annuity sounds and looks much like a corporate bond, bank term deposit, or a guaranteed investment certificate. That is, with both an annuity and a term deposit you give a financial company a lump sum in exchange for regular distributions of income. And while it is true there are similarities between these instruments—in that you pay something today in exchange for some interest income in the future—there are also some very important differences between conventional interest-bearing instruments and these insurance products. (In fact, if you are familiar with payout rates for these types of conventional instruments, you will have noticed this in Exhibits 6.1 and 6.2.)

How so? Let's say your remaining life expectancy is 30 years and you want to provide income for yourself over that period. If you tried to purchase a bond that pays you $1,000 per month for 30 years, you would actually need to pay much more than the costs listed in Exhibit 6.1. Stated another way, your investment return is actually much greater with the annuity than with the bond—as long as you are alive. For example, in today's economic environment, a term deposit of $100,000 might pay 2 or 3 percent interest per year—while an annuity might pay 7, 8, 9, or even 10 percent, depending on how old you are. But you have to give something up if you don't survive, and what you give up with an annuity is the funds you used to purchase it: as we've said, the life annuity purchase decision is a one-way street. Moreover, the type of life annuity you see in Exhibit 6.1 is illiquid and can't be cashed (ever). Remember that all you get is income—there is nothing remaining at the end of your life.

This is one of the main ways in which annuities differ from bonds and term deposits. With a bond or term deposit, you have lent capital to an institution, which pays it back to you over time, with interest, and you can cancel (or cash out the value of your investment) at any time. With an annuity, there's no cashing-out possibility; there's just income during your lifetime (or until the end of your guarantee period, if applicable).

Is the Annuity Gamble Worth It?

We understand that most people, and especially retirees, are very hesitant to enter into the gamble of a life annuity and give up the liquidity of their investments—because they fear losing control or believe they can do better with other investment alternatives.

Oddly enough, though, when people within a traditional defined benefit (DB) pension plan are coaxed to switch into a money purchase defined contribution (DC) pension plan and give up the implicit life annuity, most turn the offer down (and some react litigiously). That is, many people appreciate having a guaranteed lifetime income as opposed to a potentially larger lump sum at the end of life—and this finding is consistent with our mention of the life-cycle model in Chapter 1, where we discovered the true value of pensions.

Now, remember that we are not advocating that retirees give up all of their retirement savings and purchase a life annuity. But if you are among those who are a little apprehensive at the thought of purchasing annuities with your retirement savings, let's explore, in more careful detail, the nature of the trade-off between retaining your investments, their market risk, and your longevity risk, versus turning your savings over to an insurance company that provides you with an annuity. We will do this with the help of a story that might sound rather odd, but please suspend your disbelief for a few minutes. The story we are about to tell has actually become rather famous in retirement planning circles.

Great-Grandma's Gamble

Imagine a 95-year-old grandmother (or great-grandmother, by now) who loves playing card games with her four best friends on Sundays. Coincidentally, all five of them are exactly 95 years old, are quite healthy, and have been retired—and playing poker together—for

30 years. Recently, however, this game has become a little tiresome, so one of the ladies has decided to juice up the group's activities. Last time they met, she proposed they each take $100 (or £100, if you like) out of their purses and put the money on the kitchen table. "Whoever survives to the end of the year gets to split the $500," she said. "If you don't make it, you forfeit the money. And one more thing: *Don't tell the kids*."

Yes, this is odd, but you will see our point in a moment.

All of the others thought this was an interesting proposal and agreed, but they felt it was risky to keep $500 on the kitchen table for a whole year. So, the five of them decided to put the money in a local bank's one-year term deposit, which was paying 5 percent interest for the year.

So, what will happen next year? According to statistics compiled by actuaries, there is a roughly 20 percent chance that any given member of Great-Grandma's poker club will pass on to the next world during the coming year. This, in turn, implies an 80 percent chance of survival. And while virtually anything can happen during the next 12 months of waiting—actually, there are 120 combinations, believe it or not—the odds imply that on average four of the members will survive to split the $525 pot ($500 from the $100 allotments plus 5 percent interest, or $25, from the bank) at year-end.

Note that each survivor will get $131.25 in exchange for her original investment of $100. The 31.25 percent investment return contains 5 percent of the bank's money and a healthy 26.25 percent of "mortality credits." These credits represent the capital and interest lost by the deceased and gained by the survivors. Exhibit 6.3 shows how the funds are distributed initially and at the end of one year.

As you can see, the nonsurvivor forfeited her claim to the funds. (This is the reason that Great-Grandma's friend warned the others not to tell the kids—because the original capital is lost, not retained by the estate.) While the beneficiaries of the nonsurvivor

Exhibit 6.3 Great-Grandma's Poker-Table Bet—How Is the Money Allocated?

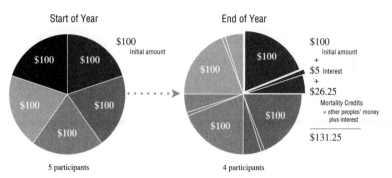

might be frustrated with the outcome, the survivors get a superior investment return. More importantly, they all got to manage their lifetime income risk in advance, without having to worry about what the future would bring.

The Power of Mortality Credits

We think (as do many others) that this story does a nice job of translating the benefits of longevity insurance into investment rates of return. Let's be clear about the benefit: there is no other financial product that guarantees such high rates of return, conditional on survival.

In fact, this story can be taken one step further. What if Great-Grandma and her poker club had decided to invest the $500 in the stock market, or even some risky energy fund for the year? Moreover, what happens if this energy fund collapses in value during the year and falls 20 percent—how much will the surviving poker players lose?

Well, if you are thinking "nothing"—that is absolutely the correct answer. They divide the $400 among the surviving four and get their original $100 back.

Such is the power of mortality credits. They subsidize losses on the downside and enhance gains on the upside. In fact, we would go so far as to say that once you wrap true longevity insurance around a diversified portfolio (by "pensionizing" a portion of your nest egg), you can actually afford and tolerate more financial risk (you'll find much more on pensionization and investment risk in Chapter 9).

Of course, life annuity contracts do not actually work in the way described earlier. In our example, Great-Grandmother's "longevity bet" contract is renewable each year, and the surviving 96-year-olds have the option to take their mortality credits and go home.

In practice, annuity contracts are for life, not one-year increments, and the mortality credits are spread out and amortized over many years of retirement. But the basic insurance economics underlying the contract are exactly as described earlier. That is, the investment return from a life annuity—the cash flow you are entitled to—is made up of three things: your money, interest, and other people's money (or mortality credits). And when some participants die and leave their money on the table (so to speak), the remaining participants benefit from those mortality credits—often significantly, especially at advanced ages.

What about 50-Year-Olds—Should They Buy Personal Pensions?

A natural next question to ponder is whether this life-roulette game would yield such high returns at younger ages, and the answer is no. We have created a table (Exhibit 6.4) that shows the implied return from an annuity at different ages. (We call this an "implied" return because it is not the kind of return you get in the stock market. Instead, as we've explained, the return from an annuity is a mix of interest income and mortality credits.)

Exhibit 6.4 What Is the Expected Investment Return from a One-Year 5 Percent Longevity Bet?

Age	End-of-Year Cash Value	Probability of Dying during Year	Probability of Surviving Entire Year	Cash Payout for Each Survivor	Investment Return for Each Survivor
50	$1,050	4/1,000	996/1,000	$1,050/996	5.5%
60	$1,050	9/1,000	991/1,000	$1,050/991	6.0%
70	$1,050	20/1,000	980/1,000	$1,050/980	7.2%
80	$1,050	52/1,000	948/1,000	$1,050/948	10.7%
90	$1,050	148/1,000	852/1,000	$1,050/852	23.2%

Source: Computations by The QWeMA Group at CANNEX based on United States Life Tables, 2009. See Notes for detailed source information

Before you look at the table, though, be aware that the math professor has taken over the microphone, and you're about to encounter some equations. Don't say we didn't warn you!

As you can see from this table, if 1,000 (unisex) 70-year-olds enter into a longevity bet contract (like Great-Grandma's poker-table bet), each contributing $1 at the start of the year, and the entire pool of funds is invested at 5 percent, then at the end of the year there is $1,050 to split among the survivors.

Using the United States as an example, according to the official statistics agencies, something like 20 of these 70-year-olds will not make it to their 71st birthday, and accordingly they will forfeit both their $1 investment and any interest it would have generated. So their money will be distributed among the 980 survivors. Using 980 survivors as our example, that leads to $1,050 / 980 = $1.07 per survivor, which is an investment return of 7.17 percent and 2.17 percent (i.e., 217 basis points) better than the 5 percent interest rate available from the bank or credit union—nothing much to write home about.

However, for an 80-year-old, looking at Exhibit 6.4 we can see that our longevity bet contract yields an investment return of 10.72 percent per survivor, and at 90, the rate of return reaches 23.19 percent. Notice how the return increases with age, so for all of you 30-year-olds out there, don't do this (unless you can pass as a 95-year-old grandmother and mix in with an older crowd).

IMMEDIATE AND DEFERRED INCOME ANNUITIES: A CLOSER LOOK

We've mentioned that you can buy annuity income starting now, or buy the annuity now but start the income later. These two options for when the income from an annuity starts are known as *immediate income annuities* and *deferred income annuities*—but it is important to note that income from an "immediate" annuity can start up to a year from the purchase date.

Beyond the names, what are the differences between these two types of annuity? So far, we've mostly focused on the immediate income annuity. But the modern deferred income annuity, or DIA, takes the concept of mortality credits to the "next level" by extending the time period between when the annuity is purchased and income begins. So while a hypothetical retiree might spend $150,000 at the age of 65 to guarantee lifetime income of $10,000 per year beginning immediately, with a deferred income annuity a (younger) 55-year-old might spend $80,000 for the same $10,000 per year, but the income would begin much later, at age 70. So in the DIA case, the same benefit of $10,000 per year is cheaper than from the immediate annuity, because it is both purchased earlier and begins later.

Either way, many choices are available. The buyer of a DIA can stipulate that he or she receive $10,000 per year guaranteed for 10, 20, or 30 years, or that the income continue to the last surviving spouse. A DIA buyer can ask for a death benefit or refund of the original premium in the event that he (or she) dies and hasn't received payments totaling the amount of the premium back. The DIA buyer can also request inflation protection so that the $10,000 increases at 1 percent, 2 percent, or even at the consumer price index (CPI). These features are all available on immediate annuities as well.

What about Interest Rates?

Okay. If 30-year-olds should wait to purchase an annuity, what about 90-year-olds—should they wait, too? We're going to answer this question by looking more closely at how interest rates affect annuity payouts.

An important takeaway from Exhibit 6.4 is that at older ages the difference, or spread, between the investment return from the longevity bet contract and the interest rate earned by the entire fund grows exponentially. It should be apparent from the exhibit that at later ages the underlying (valuation) interest rate (which determines the interest component of the payment you receive) is only a small factor in determining or influencing the outcome.

Thus, it would be silly for a 90-year-old, for example, to say: "I don't want to participate in this longevity bet agreement because interest rates are quite low right now. I'll wait for a few years until they recover to historical levels."

What's wrong with this delaying strategy? First of all, you can see from our table that by the age of 90 most of the investment return comes from other people's money (the mortality credits). Second, if what our fictional 90-year-old cares about is having the greatest amount of income while she is still alive with the least amount of investment risk, the comparable alternative to an annuity—placing the money in a 5 percent term deposit—is much worse! (Again, this argument applies to a theoretical longevity bet that is renewed each year, as opposed to life annuities, which are locked up for life, but as we've said, a similar argument for life annuities can be made and is valid.)

Now, there are two important things to note about mortality credits. First, as we've now said several times, once you purchase a life annuity, you can no longer cash in or sell the insurance contract. Thus, even though the mortality-adjusted rates of return from an annuity might be very high, it is impossible to separate the mortality credits from the fixed-income instrument. Second, it's important to note that in the real world (not Great-Grandma's kitchen) many people buy joint-life annuities, which pay as long as one of the two members of the couple are still living, and which offer some guarantee periods. Both of these features reduce the mortality credits until advanced ages.

In summary, at advanced ages it is very hard to beat the implied longevity yield from a life annuity, and the underlying interest rate (or valuation rate) is only a minor part of the total return. And, as may be obvious by now, the importance of mortality credits increases with the age at which you buy the annuity. We'll revisit this concept of the implied longevity yield in detail in Chapter 12.

How Can I Use Annuities to Protect against Inflation?

In Chapter 1, we described an inflation-indexed life annuity (one in which payments go up over time because the payment amounts are matched to some index of costs or prices, such as the CPI) as the equivalent of a personal pension purchased on the open market.

And in Chapter 4, we reviewed the threat posed by inflation—and how it can ravage retirement income over time. Now, you may be wondering whether you can use annuities to protect yourself against the impacts of inflation.

The answer is yes: one way to protect yourself from the corrosive effects of inflation is to purchase an escalating income annuity. With this type of payout annuity, your payments will be adjusted upward every year by anywhere from 1 percent to 5 percent, depending on your initial request. For example, your first year's payment might be $1,000, while the next year's payment will be $1,010, and so on. This way, you can keep up with inflation as long as there are no big surprises or changes to inflation. In fact, if you want even more protection from inflation, you may be able to purchase a payout annuity that has increases based on the actual inflation rate each year.

Of course, as you might suspect, nothing is free in life, and you will have to pay for these increases by taking a reduced benefit up front. Thus, although your payments will go up over time, the initial payment will start at a much lower level. The higher the rate at which your payment increases each year, the lower your initial payment will be.

Unique and Personal Insurance

After all that, here's our main message about annuities: personal pensions, or life annuities, provide a unique and peculiar kind of insurance. They are virtually the only insurance policies that people acquire and actually hope to use! While we are all willing to pay for home insurance, disability insurance, and car insurance, we never actually want to use the policy. After all, who wants their house to burn down, leg to break, or car to crash? But the "insurable event" underlying pension annuities (the event that causes the insurance to pay out) is being alive.

Perhaps this is why the financial services industry has yet to achieve the level of success in marketing and selling these products that it has with other forms of insurance—it's still too accustomed to scaring us. In addition, retirees may focus too narrowly on the investment characteristics of an annuity, which makes them seem risky because the payoff depends on an uncertain date of death, rather than focusing on the valuable insurance component of an annuity, which guarantees your capacity to spend over your lifetime. We hope that simple tales like "Great-Grandma's Gamble" can help prospective retirees and their financial advisers understand the benefits, risks, and returns involved with buying longevity insurance.

To be sure, annuities are not a risk-free way to invest. One of the risks annuity purchasers face is related to the solvency, or creditworthiness, of the issuer. (This is also true if you have a DB pension with an employer, as you are exposed to some risk associated with the financial health of the company.) If you are planning on purchasing an annuity, you will probably want to check out the credit rating of the issuing company. You should also check and confirm how your annuity payments may be insured, which will depend on where you live, among other factors.

When you make an annuity purchase decision, you will need to consider many issues—timing of the purchase, what features to add, and which company to buy from. We know we haven't covered all of these issues. Our intention is to provide a basic overview of how immediate and deferred life annuities work and why you might want to add them to your retirement income plans. Next, we'll run through a brief overview of traditional mutual fund and stock accounts, to see where they fit in the retirement income spectrum.

7

A Review of Traditional Investment Accounts

Reading through this book until now, you might have gotten the (wrong) impression that we are not big fans of common stocks, government bonds, exchange-traded funds (ETFs), mutual funds, and traditional diversification, since we haven't had much (good) to say about them. If you recall, we pointed out how risky they can be and how a run of bad luck with these investments—at the wrong time—can practically ruin your retirement. But does that mean you should avoid them outright? Well, the fact is that nothing could be further from the truth. Although we haven't yet discussed precisely how conventional investment products fit in a pensionized portfolio, let us make it clear that they should be at the core of a properly structured retirement income plan.

Thus, although we are advocates of product allocation, we don't want to downplay or ignore the importance of traditional asset allocation. And if we are guilty of downplaying the classical instruments of financial planning, it is because they are ubiquitous, well understood, and widely described by other sources. In other words, we don't want to bore you with something you probably already know.

Recall that the main point we are trying to make in this book is that all current, future, and soon-to-be retirees should allocate their financial (capital) nest egg across more than just stocks, bonds, cash, and commodities. No matter how diversified your investments are, diversification and asset allocation are not enough to protect you against the many other risks of retirement.

As you saw in Chapter 5, we believe that retirement wealth should be allocated across three distinct silos. One silo is filled with what we can think of as pension annuities, which we have just discussed at length. For those who are lucky enough to have DB pensions, that silo is most likely covered. For those who are in DC plans, or worse, for those who have no pensions at all—you'll probably need to get some pension income. Another silo is made up of hybrid retirement income products, a product class we turn to in the next chapter. The final silo is filled with precisely the conventional instruments, like stocks, bonds, mutual or unit funds, and exchange-traded funds, which you are probably most familiar with from your retirement savings days. In contrast to the other two silos, the income portion from this silo is created by you—not by the product manufacturer, the insurance company, or the bank. Instead, you determine how much you want to withdraw using a systematic withdrawal plan, or SWP. The bottom line from all of our discussions of silos is that to get a perfect retirement income plan you should allocate your nest egg across all three.

Here's our message once again just so it's clear: the SWP portion of your retirement portfolio should contain all the stocks, bonds, cash, mutual funds, ETFs, and other vehicles that you have been using to accumulate wealth during your years of saving for retirement. There's absolutely no reason to stop using these instruments since the benefits of broad diversification and equity ownership remain important over your entire life cycle. So don't fire your stock broker if you pensionize your nest egg—at least not on our account!

Asset Allocation in Your SWP

Now that we've said you should retain all your existing investment vehicles, you may be wondering whether you should retain them in the same proportions and allocations. Here's where we have something more to say. We believe the actual asset allocation within your SWP silo should be more conservative (i.e., have more bonds) during retirement than your normal balanced asset allocation before retirement. So, if your mutual fund or ETF portfolio had 70 percent stocks and 30 percent bonds before retirement, you should probably reduce this to, say, 50 percent stocks and 50 percent bonds as you transition into retirement.

But why do we suggest a more conservative asset allocation in your SWP account in retirement? There are two very important reasons for this. Number one is rather obvious: you are getting older and, hence, you should probably have a more conservative portfolio, all else being equal. That part is straightforward. The second reason, however, is more subtle.

As we've said, we will discuss later on in this part the hybrid investment products that combine the upside of equity markets with some pension-like downside protection. As a general rule, if you use these products, you should ensure that the aggressive part of your allocation is covered by the hybrid product. That is, let the protected (insured) silo take on the risks, and be more conservative with your naked (unprotected) investments.

For example, imagine you have $600,000 in your nest egg. You want to pensionize some of your assets, and you'd like a 50/50 stock versus bonds asset allocation in the nonpensionized income silos. If you are comfortable using $200,000 to purchase a personal pension or life annuity and would like to split the remaining $400,000 evenly between stocks and bonds, you could do it in the following way: include the safest assets in the SWP component (say $200,000) and then invest the other $200,000 of your equity quota in a hybrid retirement income product. In other words, keep the SWP safe and let the insurance company protect the equities. And if the insurance company you choose doesn't allow you to have 100 percent of your hybrid retirement income product in equities (and restricts you, let's say, to only $150,000 in our example)—then take on the maximum allowable equity exposure and allocate $150,000 to bonds and $50,000 to equity in the SWP silo (to keep your overall allocation to 50/50 stocks and bonds).

Some of you might wonder if you should think about the allocation to your pension or annuity silo as if it were a bond; after all, in practice it behaves more like fixed income than a stock or market-based instrument. And that is true to a certain extent, but remember that treating pensions and annuities as bonds, and leaving the discussion there, ignores the many other important aspects of longevity insurance and protection provided by that silo, as we've just reviewed.

In sum, we are not advocating that you be too conservative in the SWP but that you should think about all three silos together when making your asset allocation decisions.

What Should You Put in the SWP?

The choices of what to put in your SWP account are virtually unlimited, and there are many creative things you can do with the asset allocation inside this account. Some retirees might want to ladder their SWP with bonds that mature at different time periods to create a synthetic income stream.

A "bond ladder" is the name given to a portfolio of bonds with different maturities. Suppose you had $50,000 to invest in bonds.

Using this approach, you could buy five different bonds, each with a face value of $10,000 (or even 10 bonds each with a face value of $5,000). Each bond, however, would have a different maturity. One bond might mature in one year, another in three years, and the remaining bonds might mature in five-plus years. Using different maturities helps you reduce the reinvestment risk associated with rolling over maturing bonds into similar fixed-income products all at once. It also helps manage the flow of money, ensuring a steady cash flow throughout the year.

Others might want to include preferred shares with higher promised (although not guaranteed) dividend yields. Some might just roll over term deposits as they come due, which is an extremely conservative strategy, and not very tax efficient if the money is sitting outside of a tax-deferred or tax-free retirement account.

As you can see, there are many possible plans of action for a SWP, and you have substantial flexibility to allocate your assets any way you see fit with this silo. In a very real sense, you have the most flexibility with your SWP compared to the other two retirement product silos. So enjoy the flexibility! This is where asset allocation shines. Just remember our advice to be a bit more conservative with this silo than you might normally like, because the third silo, hybrid retirement income, will take more risk (backed by the insurance company). And we're going to take a closer look at that third silo in the next chapter.

8

Introducing the Third Silo—Annuities with Guaranteed Living Benefits

We have discussed pensions and annuities in considerable detail. We've also provided a brief overview of the nonguaranteed (i.e., stock and bond) silo, which is likely how you've saved for retirement so far. Now we are going to spend a little more time looking at another way to get guaranteed lifetime income, through the "hybrid" silo of retirement income products that provide both lifetime income and exposure to financial markets.

Guaranteed living benefits, or GLBs, were first introduced in variable annuity (VA) contracts in the late 1990s to allow the owner to receive lifetime income, often without having to "annuitize" the contract (i.e., lock the payments in for life). The two most popular living benefits are the guaranteed lifetime withdrawal benefit (GLWB) and the guaranteed minimum income benefit (GMIB). Both of these optional riders, added onto VA contracts, allow for the potential for growth in an up market, incentives for delaying income, and a modest lifetime payout. More recently, another form of hybrid product, the fixed indexed annuity with a guaranteed living benefit, has emerged as a way to create retirement income.

Before we go any further, let's pause for a moment to define our terms here—after all, we've just spent Chapter 6 telling you all about life annuities. What are variable and fixed indexed annuities, and how are they different?

In brief, a variable annuity is an insurance contract that guarantees a minimum payment at the end of the accumulation stage. In the United States, variable annuities were first introduced in 1952 as a form of tax-deferred vehicle to fund pension arrangements. However, it wasn't until the late 1990s that insurance companies began to offer variable annuity products with income guarantees as a way to fill the gap left by the decline in defined benefit (DB) pension plans.

Building on the basic variable annuity chassis, variable annuities with guaranteed living income benefits are a relatively new entrant to the retirement income landscape—and these products are now available or are poised to become available from insurance companies around the globe—with current sales in the United States, United Kingdom, Canada, and Australia, and variable annuity products now in development for the New Zealand market.

As we've said, at the most basic level, VAs with GLBs are like a mutual fund (or other nonguaranteed investment) that also includes a rider that ensures the owner can receive income from their VA for life, no matter how the underlying investments perform.

That is, as one example, if you purchase a variable annuity with a guaranteed living income benefit for $100,000 with a 5 percent income rider, you are guaranteed to receive $5,000 (nonindexed) per year for the rest of your life—even if the value of your underlying investments goes down, even all the way to zero. While the first versions of these products typically limited withdrawals to a maximum of 20 years, the current crop provides lifetime income, and typically, variable annuities provide an income stream of 5 percent of the base amount.

Similarly, a fixed indexed annuity, or FIA, is also an insurance contract, with the tax-deferred annual interest linked to a stock market benchmark, most commonly (in the United States) the Standard & Poor's (S&P) 500. With an FIA, insurers promise to protect buyers against market losses but "cap" or limit any upside gain they pay. When a guaranteed living benefit is added to an FIA, the result is quite similar to a VA with a GLB. Today, the FIA plus GLB combination is growing in popularity, but the use of this product combination to provide lifetime income in retirement is still relatively new.

Guarantees and Growth: How Variable Annuities with Guaranteed Living Income Benefits Work

How do these products work, and how do you know how much money you will get each year? In many ways, these products are like mutual or unit funds because the products underlying the products are, in fact, mutual funds. Technically, they are a form of mutual fund known, depending on where you live, as a segregated fund, a separate account, or a separately managed account. These are investment funds that combine the growth potential of a mutual fund with the security of a life insurance policy—and accordingly they are often referred to as mutual funds with an insurance policy wrapper. "Seg funds" or separately managed accounts offer certain guarantees, such as reimbursement of capital upon death, and are purchased through financial advisers. As required by law, these funds are fully segregated, or held separately, from the company's general investment funds, hence their name.

Back to VAs with guaranteed living income benefits. Let's say you invest $100,000 in a VA with GLB. On the day that you make your purchase, the "contract value" (that is, the market value of your investment) and the "guaranteed withdrawal base" (that is, the amount used to calculate the income payments—also called the protected value) are both $100,000. For the rest of your life, you are now guaranteed (like with an annuity) to receive 5 percent (or $5,000) in annual income from your investment. Your annual payment is always calculated from that guaranteed withdrawal base.

But that's just the income side. At the same time, the money you use to buy your VA with GLB is invested in mutual funds available from the issuer. This balance (the contract value) will fluctuate from day to day, based on the value of the underlying mutual funds. Ordinarily, you might not care about the contract value—after all, your income is calculated based on the guaranteed withdrawal base. However, these products provide some upside potential if markets rise, and here's how: if your invested funds do well and the contract value exceeds the value of the withdrawal base, then that withdrawal base can be reset to the new, higher level. Most VAs with GLBs allow the withdrawal base to be reset once every three years, and this process is often called a "step up" benefit.

In addition to step up resets, there is yet another way to increase the income you get from a VA with GLB. Let's say you buy a VA with GLB product before you retire and need the income. What happens then? If you buy a VA with GLB but delay making withdrawals, then an "income credit" is added to the withdrawal base annually, usually 5 percent. When you begin receiving payments from your VA with GLB, they will be calculated using the new, higher withdrawal base.

For example, if you purchase a VA with GLB for $100,000 with a 5 percent (simple) income credit and delay making any withdrawals for two years, the guaranteed withdrawal base will be your original investment + year one's income credits + year two's income credits, or ($100,000) + ($100,000 × 5 percent = $5,000) + ($100,000 × 5 percent = $5,000) = $110,000. Your annual payments will be $110,000 × 5 percent = $5,500, not $5,000, because you delayed your withdrawals for two years. And if you delay your withdrawals for five years, your guaranteed withdrawal base will grow to $125,000 and your

Exhibit 8.1 Delaying Withdrawals from a VA with GLB with 5 Percent Simple Income Credit (and No Step-Ups)

	Start Withdrawals Immediately	Start Withdrawals after Two Years	Start Withdrawals after Five Years
Guaranteed Withdrawal Base	$100,000	$110,000	$125,000
Annual Payments	$5,000	$5,500	$6,250

annual payout will be $6,250 ($125,000 × 5 percent—note again that this is simple, not compound interest). (This is a little like the deferred annuities we discussed earlier, in Chapter 6.) Remember, you benefit from this higher withdrawal regardless of the performance of the investments you hold inside the VA with GLB. And if your guaranteed withdrawal base is reset during the delay period, the income credit is calculated on that new, stepped-up base.

Exhibit 8.1 provides a table that shows what we've just said, to make sure it's clear.

It's important to note that income credits to the guaranteed withdrawal base are not cashable or available to you. You still own the underlying assets in a VA with GLB and can cash them out if you like, but the income credit does not increase the contract value, only the guaranteed withdrawal base. For this reason, we like to call these "phantom income credits"—because they are not a real, cashable benefit, but (like a phantom) something with no physical reality. For example, if you delay withdrawals as we have just explained, so that you are now withdrawing $6,250 on a guaranteed withdrawal base of $125,000—and then you decide you would like to collapse your VA with GLB and withdraw all your funds—you will receive the market value of your investment (less costs and fees), not the VA with GLB withdrawal base of $125,000.

At the same time, the value of your portfolio may go down as funds are withdrawn through your regular income payouts, but these withdrawals do not affect the guaranteed withdrawal base—just the contract value. So there are two values which the owner of a VA with GLB will want to track: the portfolio (or contract) value and the guaranteed withdrawal base.

After all that, you can see that these products are like life annuities because they provide the purchaser with a guaranteed lifetime income stream. They are also a bit like life annuities for the issuer, who hopes to benefit by pooling the risks of all the purchasers. That is, those who pay the rider fees finance the income stream for those who exceed average life expectancy and have no money left in their own portfolio values. But unlike annuities, you own the investment assets in your VA with GLB, which you can withdraw at any time (subject to redemption fees, taxes, and other charges).

We'll look at the costs to pensionize your nest egg using different products in a moment. But how much are the fees for a VA with GLB? In exchange for the guaranteed income and phantom income credits available through a VA with GLB, you need to pay higher fees for these products compared to annuities or mutual funds. A typical annual fee ranges from as little as 100 basis points (1 percent) to as much as 500 basis points (5 percent), depending on what market you are in, the fund choices in your VA, and whether you select all the available bells and whistles.

Evaluating an Annuity with Guaranteed Living Benefits: How Should You Choose?

Let's say you've reviewed your retirement income options and you're interested in exploring whether the products in this silo are the right choice for you. How should you decide between your available options? At a very general level, you will need to consider the following factors:

- Basic features of the issuing company, such as their credit rating, and basic features of the available contract, including contract types (single life or joint life), minimum and maximum deposits, sales charges, and expenses.

- Your options for receiving income from the product, including when income can start, how much you can receive, and how waiting to start receiving income might affect the amount.

We are not advocating the purchase of any particular one of these products, or even suggesting any one feature is more important than another. Obviously, if you decide to include a VA with GLB or an FIA with GLB (or an immediate or deferred income annuity) in your retirement income strategy, you will need to do your own due diligence and work with a financial adviser to choose the product and features that are most important and relevant to you.

At the same time, the retirement income landscape—particularly for products in this silo—is constantly evolving, with new products, issuers, and features emerging over time. We are not suggesting the information about this silo is valid for your individual situation, or for future annuity products, or even for the retirement income products that have yet to emerge. We are suggesting products from this silo can fill in an important piece of the retirement income puzzle, and our intention is to get you thinking about how (and if) they can work for you.

In the next section, now that we've gone over the available products for generating retirement income, we are going to start to provide a fundamental theory of retirement income planning. This theory will allow you to bring retirement income products together to build a coherent plan for your future. Ready? Read on.

9

Your Retirement Sustainability
Fundamental Concepts in Retirement Income Planning

We have now reviewed the main categories, or silos, of retirement income, and we've discussed why you will want to protect yourself against the new risks you face as you approach retirement.

In the coming chapters, we are going to start to tell you how to put it all together using a couple of different case studies, and we are going to take you through a step-by-step process to pensionize your nest egg. But these last few chapters of Part Two set the stage and provide the theoretical background for pensionizing your nest egg.

Accordingly, you might find this to be the toughest part of the book to slog through—but we believe the effort will pay off (literally) for you. To break up the task a bit, as we go along we've provided background and definitions of all the main concepts we're asking you to work through.

In this chapter we are going to start by looking at retirement income planning from a new perspective. In this first section, we want to draw a distinction between financial economics and financial planning. Now, we are oversimplifying the distinction, but in general terms, a financial economist asks, "What resources do you have?" while a financial planner asks, "What lifestyle do you want?"

As you read through this next section, imagine you can choose from one of two sets of reading glasses to help make the text (and the ideas) clear. On one hand, there are the financial economics glasses, and on the other, there are the financial planning glasses—and we're going to ask you to put on one or the other as we work through this section. (Take a look at Exhibit 9.1 for a visualization of these ideas.)

You can see that both the financial economics approach and the financial planning approach agree that pensionization is optimal; they just follow different paths to reach the same conclusion. The financial economics approach is concerned with lifetime

Exhibit 9.1 Two Views of Your Finances: Financial Economics versus Financial Planning

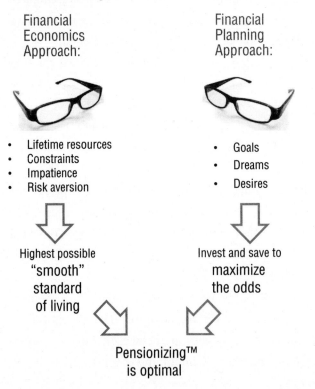

Financial Economics Approach:

- Lifetime resources
- Constraints
- Impatience
- Risk aversion

Highest possible "smooth" standard of living

Financial Planning Approach:

- Goals
- Dreams
- Desires

Invest and save to maximize the odds

Pensionizing™ is optimal

resources, constraints, risk aversion, and impatience—while the financial planning approach focuses on goals, dreams, and desires. The economists want to smooth your standard of living over time, while the planners want to invest and save to maximize the chance of your investing and retirement success.

Now, this slightly fanciful discussion of reading glasses may seem a bit removed from the practical concern of providing retirement income for life, but stick with it. The implications for structuring your retirement income, and for understanding the role of pensions in your future, are very real!

Which Glasses Will You Wear?

You may recall that in Chapter 1 we described the life-cycle model of consumption, which provides a way to measure the true value of a pension. That is, we said that the true value of a pension can be represented by what people would pay to buy it on the open market.

The life-cycle model also gives us a useful way to think about planning for retirement. At its most basic formulation, life-cycle economics is concerned with how to spread, or smooth, your financial resources and spending over your entire lifetime. According to this framework, during your economically productive years you build up wealth so you can spend it in your old age.

HUMAN CAPITAL AND YOUR PERSONAL BALANCE SHEET

Your personal balance sheet—which is a one-page snapshot that summarizes everything you owe and everything you own—contains two types of assets: visible and invisible.

The visible assets are items like houses, cars, bank accounts, and retirement savings accounts.

(continued)

The invisible asset is what economists call "human capital." It is the sum total of all the money you will earn in the future (after tax). Think of it as the human equivalent of oil and gold reserves that are deep underground and might take years to extract.

Technically, your human capital value is estimated by adding up the present value of the salary, wages, and income you will earn over the course of your entire working life.

This is the value of your human capital—and for many people in the early stages of life, it can be worth millions of dollars.

While you age, work, and save a fraction of your earnings, the value of your human capital declines as the number of years you expect to spend in the labor force goes down. So from a life-cycle point of view, we could define "retirement" as the point at which your human capital is largely depleted, you have stopped generating dividends from it, and you have begun to consume the financial resources you have saved up over time.

How Many Eggs Can You Withdraw from Your Nest?

Viewed in this way, the main challenge of retirement planning is to make sure you have enough resources saved up from the economically productive part of the life cycle (your working years) to spread, or smooth, over the remainder of your life span (that is, from the point of retirement until you die). This goal is more difficult than it might sound: as we saw in Part One, simply setting aside money—whether in T-bills, term deposits, or a diversified portfolio of stocks and bonds—does not mean it will be there, in real terms (that is, after adjusting for the effects of inflation), when you need it. So, given that uncertainty, how do you know how much you need to save? How will you know when you've saved enough?

SMOOTHING YOUR LIFETIME CONSUMPTION

Over the years, researchers and scholars in the field of financial economics have developed a set of guidelines outlining how rational individuals should spend their total wealth over their entire lifetime. These are often described as guidelines for "consumption smoothing."

Among other things, these guidelines imply that saving a fixed percentage of your income (say 5 percent, 10 percent, or 15 percent) isn't as important as ensuring that your standard of living is relatively stable over time.

So, if saving 10 percent this year will result in a dramatically lower standard of living compared to what you expect to have next year, or the year after, then don't save. Instead, focus on maintaining a smooth standard of living—as opposed to a smooth saving rate.

How does this apply to retirement income planning?

When you are setting your retirement income goals and objectives, make sure you are not targeting a standard of living that is much higher than your current (pre-retirement) standard of living. There is no point in starving yourself during your working years just so that your income and lifestyle jumps at retirement—or alternately, in assuming that your expenses will drop dramatically merely by virtue of the fact that you are no longer working. Instead, be realistic. Smooth your consumption.

The answers to these questions will depend, not surprisingly, on how much you intend to spend in retirement. And here is where life-cycle thinking can be used to help shed light on planning your spending as you progress through your retirement. Before we go any further, let's take a moment to delve into a discussion on how to generate income from your nest egg in retirement—looking in particular at the concept of safe withdrawal rates.

Retirement planning literature is full of discussions about how much retirees can afford to withdraw from their portfolios each year without unduly drawing down the capital. Many financial advisers (wearing financial planner glasses, naturally) have argued that the maximum initial portfolio withdrawal rate should be in the range of 4 to 5 percent of your nest egg. This is described as the "safe withdrawal rate," and those planning for retirement are cautioned not to exceed it. However, one notable aspect of this discussion is that the safe rate is assumed to be constant over time. Thus, the rate, not the amount, is the same whether you are 65, 75, or even 85.

But is that really rational? Here's where the life-cycle model steps in. (Financial economist glasses on, please.) Instead of targeting a fixed standard of living or constant portfolio withdrawal rate when you are spreading your resources over your lifetime, you should set aside fewer dollars to be consumed at older ages. Looking at this issue wearing the financial economics glasses, you would be willing to sacrifice income at the age of 100 in exchange for more income at the age of 80, and even more at age 70. And why is that? Because if you are 70, your probability of surviving to 100 is less than your probability of surviving to age 80. Thus, giving the ages of 100 and 80 equal weight in your planned spending is illogical—although that's precisely what the notion of a constant safe withdrawal rate suggests.

Now, you may be thinking that smoothing your income suggests adopting a constant safe withdrawal rate in retirement. However, relative to pensionizing, we are arguing that a constant withdrawal rate actually wastes resources if you die early. In contrast, a life annuity is better at creating a smooth income stream without leaving any leftovers. And more importantly, in the absence of annuities you should smooth consumption, taking into account the probability you will be around to enjoy the consumption. You will recall that we explored survival probabilities earlier, in Chapter 2, when we showed the chance of living to different ages. What we are saying here is a natural outcome of that first conversation. That is, it makes the most sense to allot more funds to the earlier years of retirement and less to the later years. This has nothing to do with spending less as you age or even with the time value of money—it has to do with rationalizing your planned spending according to the probability you'll be alive to need it!

What Should You Protect Against: Floods or Meteorites?

Here's another analogy in case our message isn't clear: in the constant withdrawal rate model, you are saying you will (plan to) draw down a constant spending level (whether 4 percent of your portfolio or some other rate) in years 1, 2, 3, 4, 5, 10, 20, 30, and so on. This is a little like setting aside two equal amounts of money every year to fix your house—one to be used if the basement floods and the other to be used if the house is hit by a meteor. While both events will require you to use the stored funds, the meteor outcome is so much less likely than the flooded basement that it doesn't make any sense to save as much money to protect yourself against it.

The same rationale applies when planning your spending in old age. Viewed through the financial economics lens, it makes most sense to set aside funds for the most likely outcome (living a few years in retirement), rather than the decreasingly likely outcome (living to a very advanced age). Now, we are not saying—as should be clear from Chapter 2—to completely discount (i.e., not save for) the possibility of living to an advanced age. What we are suggesting is that there is an optimal way to make sure income is available at an advanced age; it has to do with pensions—and we will get to precisely how in just a minute.

Do You Feel Lucky? Pensions, Survival Probabilities, and Spending in Retirement

Now, in addition to the survival probabilities we've just reviewed, how you allocate your resources in retirement will also depend on your personal willingness to tolerate longevity risk. What are we talking about? If you are worried about funding a long life, you will set aside more resources to fund those later years of consumption. However, if you are willing to assume the chance of living a long life, you will set aside fewer resources.

You may recognize the trade-off we've just touched on. This is a variation of the risk-reward conversation you probably had while building your nest egg portfolio. The portfolio version of this conversation is as follows: if you can tolerate more risk (measured as portfolio volatility, or movements up and down in the value of your financial assets), you can invest differently than a risk-averse investor—and you may be rewarded with greater returns. In this case, however, the risk is that you will live to an advanced age (which is perhaps a reward in itself!), and what you are tolerating is not old age itself, but random and unknown life expectancy.

Pensions Change the Game

Okay. We've now laid the groundwork to talk about pensions and the life-cycle model. Everything we've just said about spending in retirement by risk-averse and risk-tolerant retirees is true if you have no pension income. But pension income changes the game—and from the life-cycle view of retirement income planning, this is the true function of pensions.

How so? Basically, in retirement, pension income acts as a buffer and allows you to consume more from your nest egg than you would in its absence. So, while you would, with no pension income, be quite worried about living beyond your savings, if you have a sufficiently large pension—or a sufficiently small gap between your pensionized income and your desired spending—the chance of living a longer life should no longer worry you. You have that (pensionized) income stream to fall back on should a long life materialize. As a result, you can deplete your (nonpensionized) wealth (with a higher spending rate) after which you will live on your pension income alone. And remember, if your retirement allocation includes some annuitized income, you will benefit from mortality credits, which will keep replenishing so long as you are alive. (If you have a high planned spending rate, no pension income, and no worries about outliving your savings, you will probably deplete your wealth faster still—but if that were the case, we suspect you would not be reading this book!)

If you have no pension income and you are worried about living a long life, you cannot deplete wealth until some very advanced age, and must draw down your wealth at a much slower rate. And when there is no pension income at all, you can never completely spend your wealth. This is a bigger problem than you think! In the complete absence of pension income, no matter how old you are, you will always be worried about spending too much. In the back of your mind you will be wondering, "What if I have five, ten, or even fifteen years to go?" Taking this logical flow to its extreme, you will always be worried that you will spend that last dollar.

The overall lesson here is that if you have both pensionized assets and an investment portfolio, then—all else being equal—the greater the amount of pension income, the more you can withdraw from your portfolio in the early years of retirement. In other words, you can afford to spend more if you have a pension! We'll say it again so it's clear: converting some of your initial nest egg into a stream of lifetime income by pensionizing it increases the amount you can spend at all ages, regardless of the exact cost of the pension annuity. Even when interest rates are low and the cost of $1 or £1 of lifetime income is high—like now—the net effect is that you can spend more. That is, you can deplete your nonpensionized nest egg because after it is gone you will have your pensionized income (so long as you have created a sufficient pensionized income stream) to sustain you. You don't need to hold back any funds in reserve.

The retirement income planning take away from all of this is that pension income boosts the amount you can withdraw from your portfolio—and this needs to be considered in evaluating the trade-off between purchasing some pension income versus retaining the funds in your retirement savings accounts. We'll get into more detail about how to make that specific trade-off and allocate funds to various retirement income products in a moment. For now, keep in mind: pensionizing increases your retirement income.

How Does Pensionization Impact Your Retirement Sustainability Quotient?

This next section is slightly more technical than the rest of this book, and we apologize for this in advance (well, at least one of us does). Nevertheless, we believe it is worth getting through as it provides a bit more rigor for the main argument in this book, namely, that you should pensionize a fraction of your nest egg at retirement.

In this section, we are going to introduce some new terms that are key in thinking and talking about retirement income planning. The first concept is the Retirement Sustainability Quotient, or RSQ. At the most basic level, creating a retirement income plan involves answering a two-part question: *How much money can I spend each year* and *for how many years can I spend it?* The RSQ provides an answer to those questions. You can think of the RSQ like a forecast of your retirement wealth: it calculates how likely it is that your desired standard of living will be sustainable, given the variability of your investments, their expected return, and the variability of your life span.

**UNDERSTANDING AND MEASURING YOUR RETIREMENT
SUSTAINABILITY QUOTIENT**

The Retirement Sustainability Quotient (RSQ) summarizes the likelihood that your current retirement income plan will last as long as you do.

The RSQ—which can be thought of as analogous to calculating the probability of precipitation on a given day—is estimated using an algorithm that takes into account many factors, including longevity tables and economic conditions, as well as personal factors like age, gender, health, and whether you have a defined benefit (DB) pension or just a savings plan (such as a DC plan or other retirement savings account).

An RSQ value can range from 100 percent (very sustainable, and very good) to 0 percent (very unsustainable, and very bad). But unlike a bad weather forecast, you can actually do something about a bad RSQ value: you can change your asset and product allocation to improve your RSQ. And more importantly, by pensionizing a fraction of your nest egg you can improve and increase your RSQ. There are many ways or methods for computing your plan's RSQ, just like there are many different ways to calculate the economic health of a country, such as gross national product (GNP), gross domestic product (GDP), infant mortality rate, life expectancy at birth, or the strength of its currency. No particular method is best or superior among economists and the same applies to RSQ calculations. However, our preferred method—and the approach we take through the entire book—can be expressed as follows:

$$RSQ = (\text{Fraction of Income that Is Pensionized}) \times 100\%$$
$$+ (\text{Fraction of Income that Is } \textit{Not} \text{ Pensionized})$$
$$\times (1 - \text{Portfolio's Probability of Ruin})\%$$

(continued)

Notice that all else being equal, the greater the fraction of your income that is pensionized, the higher is your RSQ. Likewise, the lower the ruin probability on the investment portfolio, the higher (and better) the RSQ score. (Your nest egg's "ruin probability" describes its vulnerability to becoming completely depleted over time.) Notice also that when the entire income is from pensionized sources, the RSQ is 100 percent, and when the entire income is from nonpensionized sources, the RSQ is 100 percent minus the probability of ruin.

So, for example, if 20 percent of your desired retirement income is coming from a guaranteed pension, and the other 80 percent is invested in a balanced portfolio (e.g., a tax-deferred account with mutual funds), which has a 30 percent probability of ruin, then your RSQ would be: 20 percent + 80 percent × (100 percent − 30 percent) = 76 percent. In contrast, if 40 percent of your desired retirement income is from a pensionized source, and the other 60 percent is at the mercy of the market, then even if the ruin probability of the portfolio is 35 percent, the RSQ would be 40 percent + 60 percent × (100 percent − 35 percent) = 79 percent, which is better than 76 percent.

One question we haven't examined is how—exactly—we get the "ruin probability" of the portfolio. This is the probability that a given spending rate will exhaust the portfolio while you are still alive. This number can be obtained analytically (using a formula) or via simulation (such as a Monte Carlo simulation). There are many commercial software packages that can do this calculation for you.

There are variations on the themes we have discussed here, but this is the basic math for understanding and computing the RSQ.

Now, it is probably obvious that the sustainability of your income in retirement is also partly a function of your spending levels (as well as your asset performance and your individual life span). And even more important than your spending level considered in isolation, is your spending level as a proportion of your total wealth. We have developed a shorthand way of talking about this proportion and refer to it as your wealth-to-needs (WtN) ratio. This ratio simply measures your total investable wealth divided by your real (inflation-adjusted) desired yearly spending. (We'll show you some specific examples in a minute.)

YOUR WEALTH-TO-NEEDS RATIO

The WtN ratio is computed by dividing two very important values into each other. The numerator (the upper or first number in your fraction) is the total amount of wealth that you have at retirement, and the denominator (the bottom number in your fraction) is the total amount you expect to require each year (or at least early on) during retirement. (Your WtN ratio will change over time, as your overall assets and desired spending change.)

To calculate your WtN ratio, divide your total wealth by the total amount you expect to need each year. If your total wealth is $1 million (for example) and the income you require is $50,000 per year, your WtN ratio is ($1,000,000 / $50,000) = 20.

If your total wealth is $500,000 and your required income is $25,000, your WtN is also 20 (as $500,000 / $25,000 also equals 20). However, if your total wealth is $500,000 and your required income is $50,000, then your WtN ratio is 10.

(continued)

You can also express your WtN ratio as a percentage. A WtN value of 25 implies a spending rate of 4 percent, while a WtN value of 50 implies a spending rate of 2 percent. (The bigger the WtN ratio, the smaller the spending rate.) You can calculate your own spending rate if you have your WtN ratio—the spending rate is simply the inverse of the ratio and is expressed as a percentage.

As you may be starting to see, the larger the WtN ratio (all else being equal) the better your financial situation.

Note that we are not including the value of human capital in this calculation; nor are we including the value of your house, or any other assets that are not intended to provide income in retirement. Remember, we've said you can define retirement as the point at which your stores of human capital are largely depleted, so this is why we aren't including a human capital value in your WtN calculation.

Now that we've introduced and defined the WtN and RSQ concepts, we are going to start to work with them. Exhibit 9.2 displays the RSQ for a generic retiree. We show the same nest egg under two very different retirement plans.

Let's pretend that generic retiree is you. One curve displays the health of your plan if you take our advice and pensionize some of your nest egg. (In the example we're going to use, one third of the income you desire in retirement is coming from pensionized sources.) The other curve shows what happens if you choose to completely ignore us and do not pensionize anything.

Now, before we look at this chart in detail, it's important to note that you already have a retirement plan (even if you've never thought about it or written anything down) and a corresponding RSQ, and how much of our inc is (will be) pensionized

Exhibit 9.2 Nest Eggs, Pensionization, and Your RSQ

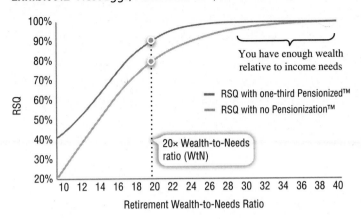

Source: Computations by The QWeMA Group at CANNEX.

you also have an existing WtN ratio—even if you've never heard this term before one minute ago.

You might want to take a moment now to give some thought to what your existing WtN and RSQ are. How healthy do you think your current retirement income plans are? We will give you a chance to calculate these numbers later on. For now, we invite you to simply speculate about where you might sit on Exhibit 9.2.

Back to the exhibit. What does it mean? The *x*-axis (running along the bottom of the chart) represents your real WtN ratio, which we explained earlier. Remember that a WtN value of 20, for example, means that your nest egg is 20 times the amount of inflation-adjusted income you would like to draw each year. The *y*-axis (running up the left-hand side of the chart) shows the RSQ at different WtN ratios.

Okay. Let's look closely at the chart. Look first at the bottom curve, labeled "RSQ with No Pensionization." As you move from lower (left) to higher (right) values of the WtN ratio, the RSQ value increases from about 20 percent to almost 100 percent. Remember, as you move from left to right, your WtN ratio is increasing—which means you have more money or are spending less.

Our chart shows that if you only have about 10 times your annual needs at retirement and no pensionized income, the sustainability of your plan is a mere 20 percent, and your retirement plan has an 80 percent chance of failure. But if your nest egg is 40 times larger than your income needs, your plan is virtually 100 percent sustainable (whether you have pensionized income or not).

It should come as no surprise that the more money you have (and the higher your WtN ratio), the more likely it is that your plan will be sustainable. In fact, if you look at the WtN value of exactly 20 on the curve with no pensionized income (which is a 5 percent spending rate), you will see that the RSQ value is approximately 80 percent. Recall that 5 percent is the maximum withdrawal rate recommended by many financial advisers and planners. But if you look at a WtN ratio of 20 with one third pensionized, you will see that the RSQ increases by a full 10 percentage points—from 80 to 90 percent.

Said another way, two retirees, each with the same-sized nest egg, the same desired income in retirement (so the same WtN ratio), and an intention to leave the same-sized financial legacy can have very different sustainability ratios. The one who pensionizes one third of her income wins the sustainability game—even though they are both withdrawing the same amount.

Pension Annuities: Step-by-Step Math

Here is a detailed example to make sure our message is apparent. If you retire with $300,000 and would like $20,000 per year of inflation-adjusted income, then this is a WtN ratio of exactly 15, which is found at the left-hand side of Exhibit 9.2.

If you (our generic retiree) pensionize $100,000 of your nest egg, you will be entitled to $6,000 of annual pensionized (annuity) income, inflation-adjusted and guaranteed for life. The other $200,000 would be used to try to generate the remaining ($20K – $6K) = $14,000 of desired income.

So one third of your desired $20,000 is assured 100 percent sustainability (as it has been pensionized). The other $14,000 must be generated from your remaining $200,000—and this spending ratio (which represents a WtN ratio of 14) has only a 50 percent sustainability value on its own, which you can see in Exhibit 9.2.

To combine the values, we take 50 percent of 14,000/20,000 and add it to 100 percent of 6,000/20,000, which we write mathematically as: 50 percent × (14,000/20,000) + 100 percent × (6,000/20,000). When you combine the two values, you arrive at the RSQ value of 65 percent.

Here is the bottom line: By ensuring one third of the income you want in retirement comes from pensionized sources, the RSQ value increases from 55 percent (with no pensionization) to 65 percent (with one-third pensionization). Why? Because you have moved money from a non-longevity-insured silo to a longevity-insured one, which increases sustainability.

Is an RSQ of 65 percent good enough? Well, it is certainly better than 50 percent. But it is well below the numbers that would make us comfortable (90 percent to 95 percent). Were this your situation, we would ultimately recommend that you try to rebudget and reduce your spending. But our point here is simply to demonstrate, at a basic level, the benefits of pensionization. We've already argued (earlier in this chapter) that pensions increase spending at all points in retirement. Here, we are adding the observation that pensionization also increases sustainability, as well as income, in retirement. We hope our message is sinking in: pension annuities keep you afloat.

The True Gift of Pensionization

Here's the main message from this section: at very high WtN ratios— when you have a lot of money relative to your income needs—your RSQ values are already close to 100 percent, and pensionization doesn't make much of a difference. (Remember, pensionization with a life annuity will impact the amount of money left as a legacy to your heirs, because this kind of pensionization is an irreversible handover of assets to the provider. If you use a hybrid retirement income product, you may be able to preserve some legacy value.)

Likewise, on the other side of the chart (at low WtN levels) the RSQ numbers are quite poor, and although pensionization does improve the situation, the numbers are still quite risky, or unsustainable.

Accordingly, the real benefit of pensionization comes in the middle region, where you can take your plan from mediocre 60 percent and 70 percent values up to very safe 90 percent (and beyond) values. This is the true gift of pensionization—it provides increased sustainability all along that middle region (not at the extremes).

Now, a moment ago we touched on the fact that pensionizing affects your financial legacy. In the next chapter, we are going to delve much more deeply into this issue—and help you answer the most difficult question we think you will face in your retirement planning.

10

The Most Difficult Question You Will Ever Have to Answer (About Your Retirement)

Before we launch into our detailed discussion of how to allocate your retirement savings to pensions and other retirement income products, we believe that you have to ask yourself a very difficult question. And, more importantly, you have to come up with an answer! Here's the question: who do you love more, yourself or the kids? Who is more important—is it you, or is it them?

Yes, of course, we know this is a very awkward subject to contemplate. And rest assured that we would never bring it up were it not for the fact that your optimal course of action is quite sensitive to the answer to this question.

Okay, let us phrase the question in slightly different, more financial, terms. Think of it this way: what is the purpose of the retirement savings account, investment portfolio, and mutual funds you have worked so diligently to accumulate over your working years? Is this money truly meant to finance your own retirement, or is your intention to leave something for the next generation? On a scale of zero to 100, what percentage of your current assets would you like to bequeath as a legacy to your family and loved ones, and what percentage would you like to spend while you are still alive?

Now, whether you have no kids or a very large and loving family, the answer to this question is by no means obvious or to be taken for granted. You may have many children and grandchildren who are grown-up, self-sufficient, and not in need of any financial assistance from you. Or let's face it—you may not really like any of them. Alternatively, even if you don't have any children, you may have a favorite charity, association, museum, or library you plan to support.

Once again we ask, "What is truly more important?" Sure, some of you might be tempted to say, "All of the above"—just like our kids (or even you!) when asked which of many options they want for dessert. But the harsh reality of economics is that we can't satisfy everyone. (Back to our financial economics glasses again.)

Now, how do you know what is the right amount to allocate to yourself, your kids, charities, or other financial legacy interests? The truth is, there is no formula for this, and no right answer. We know you may have to grapple with this a bit. Work through some different scenarios and perhaps consult with your spouse or a trusted adviser. At this point, however, you don't need to come up with a final answer. In Part Three, when we take you through the steps of pensionizing your nest egg, you will be able to see the trade-offs between increasing and decreasing the amounts you want to allocate to yourself (sustainable income in retirement) and your financial legacy. Right now, we are just inviting you to speculate about the overall division of your retirement wealth between your sustainable retirement income on one hand, and your financial legacy on the other. So, if your answer is 50/50 (you versus them), or 25/75, or 75/25 (or even 100/0 or 0/100), just give it your best shot.

Here's where we're going with this: depending on your preference for one over the other, your entire retirement plan and optimal product allocation will be very different. If, for example, you are willing to sacrifice some of your own spending while you are alive so that you create a financial legacy after you are gone, then the types of products you should be holding revolve around life insurance and other instruments that pay more when you are no longer around, but earn less while you are alive. However, if you are more concerned about maximizing the amount of sustainable income you can receive during your lifetime, your plan will allocate more assets to income or lifetime payout annuities and variable annuities with guaranteed living income benefits, and decrease allocations to life insurance and a SWP account.

Retirement Sustainability or Financial Legacy?

The upshot of this discussion is that your desire for a financial legacy—on a scale of zero to 100—is just as important as your risk aversion or tolerance in determining your asset allocation. Remember how the financial industry (properly) counsels very risk-averse investors to stay away from risky stocks and mutual funds or unit trusts? Well, the exact same thing applies to product allocation in retirement. Those who have no concern for leaving a financial legacy should lean toward pensionization, while those who have a very strong preference for creating a financial legacy and little fear of outliving their assets should not pensionize their nest egg.

Exhibit 10.1 provides a graphical illustration of this trade-off. You must decide where you would like to live on this retirement frontier (which is a curve on a graph showing the range of optimal allocations). You can't be in two places at once, and you can't avoid the frontier. So where would you like to sit? This exhibit is designed to illustrate the variability in product allocation associated with different points along the frontier. So, for example, a retiree who wants to maximize sustainability (in the lower right-hand corner) might have life annuities or variable annuities with a guaranteed living benefit, stocks, and bonds—while the retiree who wants to maximize their financial legacy (at the top left) might have only stocks and bonds. We illustrated these different allocations using different shades of gray in our exhibit.

Exhibit 10.1 The Conceptual Retirement Income Frontier

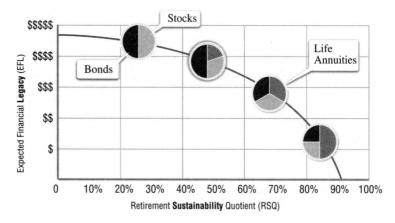

Pricing Your Inheritance

We've just introduced another concept that directly affects your retirement income plans—and that is what we call your expected financial legacy, or EFL. This value measures, in today's dollars, the financial legacy you can expect to leave from your retirement savings. (Recall that in this case, we are using "expected" in its mathematical sense—to mean the probability-weighted average of all possible values.) It is different from a future value, such as an expected death benefit from a life insurance policy. Instead, it measures, in current dollars, the expected value of your financial legacy (see our technical glossary for a refresher on this point). The power of this concept is that it allows you to compare your legacy and your nest egg in an apples-to-apples comparison. If your nest egg is $800,000 and your EFL is $400,000, then you know that you are really using only about 50 percent of your nest egg at any given time to supplement your desired retirement income, and your legacy value shows the equivalent of about half of the current amount left.

EXPECTED FINANCIAL LEGACY

When you die, your family and loved ones and your favorite charity will inherit your assets. These assets make up your financial legacy.

However, it is very hard to predict (when you are alive) exactly what that financial legacy will be (when you pass on). If you live a long time and spend a lot during retirement, you won't leave much—if any—financial legacy.

The expected financial legacy (EFL) estimates what that legacy will be in present value terms (that is, what it is worth today). It is generated using an algorithm that takes into account your health, wealth, and desired living standards, among other variables.

You can increase your EFL by purchasing life insurance (for the death benefit), by spending less in retirement, perhaps by investing more aggressively for higher returns, or you can shorten your life (not recommended!).

Here is a more specific example to help you understand this trade-off.

Imagine you would really like to leave your favorite grandson $100,000 as an inheritance. One possibility is to just give him the money right now. That will obviously cost you $100,000, but it won't quite achieve your goal of giving him an inheritance, which implies something that occurs at a later date—hopefully much later.

Another possibility is to set aside $40,000 today in a zero-coupon bond that matures in 20 years at a value of $100,000. A zero-coupon bond, as its name indicates, is a bond that pays no interest (that is, you don't receive any payments while you hold the bond) and grows in value over time until it matures at par. If you pay $40,000 for a zero-coupon bond, your favorite grandkid will get $100,000 in 20 years. Now, that might be too long for you (or him) to wait. After all, if you want Johnny to get the check when they are reading your final will and testament, buying a zero-coupon bond can misfire on you by decades.

The most efficient way to ensure that Johnny gets $100,000 when you are being lowered into the ground is by going to an insurance company today and buying a single-premium life insurance policy that pays a death benefit of exactly $100,000 to the beneficiary (Johnny) just as you are moving on to a better place. The cost of this policy at the age of 65 is approximately $15,000, which is much less than (the inefficient) $40,000 for a zero-coupon bond and certainly much less than a $100,000 lump sum (if you give him the money today).

Now, bear with us here for a moment.

If Johnny was absolutely certain that he was going to inherit $100,000 from you upon your demise, he could actually go to an investor and sell his inheritance today. Sure, there might be some technicalities since you could change your mind and the investor might not trust you or Johnny, but in theory it would be possible for Johnny to monetize his inheritance right now. And guess how much he could get? Probably the same $15,000 you would have to pay for the insurance policy. Think about it: this is financial economics at work—every plan has a price, and every payoff can be quantified.

Thus, the EFL of $100,000 at death is $15,000 today. If you want to leave Johnny $200,000, then the current EFL is $30,000—and any economist will agree.

Finding Your Spot on the Frontier

Let's take this thinking to the next level. If you plan to leave your entire estate—house, car, stable of horses, or retirement savings portfolio—to Johnny, this too has an EFL today. It might not be as easy to compute as the $100,000 death benefit because you don't know exactly what you will leave at a random time of death, but it can and should be done.

Now, you may be wondering: how does the Retirement Sustainability Quotient (RSQ) mesh with the EFL? What we have said is that every financial plan has both a legacy value and a sustainability value. However, as you've noticed, we don't measure both values using the same scale: the RSQ is a percentage value and the EFL is a dollar amount. How do these two values work together?

Perhaps another way to think about RSQ and EFL is like evaluating a car based on its fuel economy, on one hand, and its horsepower, on the other: two different measures of how suitable the car is for your needs. And just like someone buying a car, you need to make sure you evaluate the trade-offs from one variable (fuel economy) on the other (horsepower).

For example, let's say you have an EFL of $500,000—what is your corresponding RSQ for the plan that gives you this expected EFL? Or let's say you have a plan with an RSQ of 80 percent—what is the EFL value at that sustainability level? Our point is that you need to measure both of these values to get the full picture of where your retirement income plans are going, so you can better plan the retirement you want. Looking at only one side of the scale is a little bit like planning with one eye closed. Both the EFL and the RSQ are important values to consider in designing your retirement income plans, and you should really take both into account.

We've already talked in some detail about the RSQ, or sustainability value. Exhibit 10.1 shows us the trade-off between the EFL and the RSQ in pictures. At the lower-right corner are plans with high sustainability but a low EFL. That is, a person with this plan has made the decision (whether deliberately or not) to prioritize sustainability over legacy: more income (while alive) instead of a higher legacy value (at death). In contrast, at the upper-left corner are plans with a high EFL. These people have made the decision to try to maximize the value of assets left to the kids at the expense of sustainability (income during their lifetimes).

What we want to illustrate is that every plan—even yours—falls somewhere on this frontier, whether you know it or not. That is, an RSQ and an EFL can be calculated for whatever plan you come up with. If you have $500,000, plan to retire in good health at age 63, and want to draw $25,000 from your portfolio each year, an RSQ and EFL can be calculated for you. And if you decide to withdraw more or less from that portfolio, a new EFL and RSQ can be calculated for each of those paths. Depending on how much more or less you plan to withdraw from your portfolio, you will move up or down the legacy/sustainability frontier—the curve in Exhibit 10.1. Traveling down the curve (toward the bottom right-hand corner) increases sustainability at the cost of legacy, while traveling up the slope (toward the upper left-hand corner) increases legacy at the cost of sustainability. We're going to look at moving up and down the frontier in much more detail in the next section.

Now, we know our discussions of the retirement income frontier are still relatively theoretical at this point. The good news is that we are going to provide you with the tools to make these calculations yourself (later, in Part Three). But right now, we are exploring a concept: the trade-off of legacy versus sustainability. Our message is that every plan for your retirement income falls at a specific point on the legacy/sustainability frontier. Don't get stuck someplace you don't want to be!

11

Divvying Up Your Nest Egg

We have now described each of the product silos in turn, and we've given you the theoretical background of retirement income planning, which we hope describes the trade-offs between sustainable income in retirement (RSQ) and your expected financial legacy (EFL).

In this chapter, we'll look at one example in more detail. Take the case of Robert ("Bob") Retiree, age 65, who is trying to determine how much he can spend from his nest egg and what impact different spending plans will have on the sustainability of his spending plans, and his financial legacy.

Creating a Retirement Plan for Robert Retiree: Cases 1 through 10

Bob initially considers a 7 percent spending rate. That is, he wonders if he can spend $7 per year for every $100 of his current nest egg. Based on where that spending rate places him on the sustainability/legacy frontier, he decides to experiment with a spending rate of $6, and then settles on a spending rate of $5.50 per $100 of nest egg.

Exhibit 11.1 shows the impact of different spending rates on the sustainability of Bob's retirement income plans and on the EFL of each spending rate. You can see that a spending rate of $7 gives him what he considers an unacceptably low RSQ (about 60 percent) coupled with a low EFL (about $7). Moving his spending down to $6 increases his RSQ to just under 70 percent and more than doubles his EFL to just under $20. Finally, shifting spending downward to $5.50 brings his RSQ up to just over 70 percent and his EFL to almost $25. You can see each of these spending plans plotted in Exhibit 11.1—as plans 1, 2, and 3. (You can also see that we have assumed his nest egg has an expected portfolio return of 3.5 percent and a volatility of 11.3 percent.)

Once Bob has settled (as a starting point) on a spending rate that gives him a baseline sustainability score of about 70 percent, he is ready to explore the impact of pensionization on his plans. In these cases, we will explore the impact of adding a lifetime payout annuity to Bob's retirement income plans. Exhibit 11.2 shows how his plans move along the sustainability/legacy frontier if he

Exhibit 11.1 Robert Retiree's RSQ and EFL with Three Spending Rates

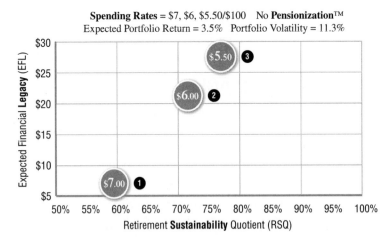

pensionizes between 10 and 40 percent of his nest egg. Take a look at cases 4 through 10 in the exhibit. You can see that increasing the pensionization of his nest egg increases the sustainability of his retirement income, but at the cost of financial legacy. At one end of the frontier, pensionizing 10 percent of his nest egg increases his sustainability score—it moves from about 77 percent (in case 3) to about 81 percent (in case 4)—while decreasing his EFL modestly (from about $28 to about $27). At the other end of the frontier, in case 9, pensionizing 40 percent of his nest egg (with a lifetime payout annuity) moves his sustainability score way up—to just under 93 percent—while decreasing his EFL to just about $23.

You'll note that there is one more case that Bob explores, and it's illustrated as case 10 on our exhibit. In this case, Bob moves up and off the frontier we have traced with cases 4 through 9 by increasing the expected return (and volatility) of his nonpensionized wealth. In case 10, he has continued to pensionize a total of 40 percent of his nest egg with a lifetime payout annuity. However, because he now

Exhibit 11.2 Robert Retiree's RSQ and EFL with Varying Levels of Pensionization

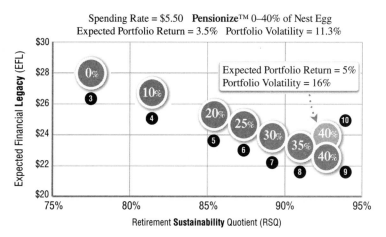

has a relatively large fraction of his investable wealth pensionized, he can afford to expose his nonpensionized assets to more investment risk, as he has the pensionized income to fall back on. The impact of moving his remaining assets to a riskier investment allocation (with a higher expected return) is to move him up and off the retirement income frontier. That is, for the same sustainability score (or at no cost to the sustainability of his income stream), he can have a higher EFL.

In Exhibit 11.3, we've displayed all of the values in table form, so it is easier to see the relationships between spending rates, pensionization, and the resulting RSQ and EFL resulting from each plan.

Exhibit 11.3 Comparing RSQ and EFL with Varying Levels of Pensionization: Ten Cases

Spending Rate = $7.00 to $5.50 Pensionize™ 0–40% of Nest Egg Expected Return = 3.5 (or 5%) Volatility = 11.3% (or 16%)			
Spending Rate per $100 ($)	**Percent of Nest Egg that Is Pensionized**	**RSQ (%)**	**EFL ($)**
7.00	Case 1	–	59.47	7.36
6.00	Case 2	–	71.37	21.33
5.50	Case 3	–	77.45	27.99
5.50	Case 4	10	81.47	26.66
5.50	Case 5	20	85.39	25.31
5.50	Case 6	25	87.30	24.62
5.50	Case 7	30	89.16	23.94
5.50	Case 8	35	90.97	23.25
5.50	Case 9	40	92.70	22.55
5.50	Case 10	40	92.72	23.84

Take a few minutes to ponder Bob's paths and plans—we're going to work through a detailed example of pensionizing a nest egg in Part Three, next.

What Is the Cost to Pensionize?

One question you may have been wondering about is: "What are the costs to pensionize?" In particular, you may have heard that some investment products are expensive, and you may question whether the value of your assets will be significantly eroded by annual fees and costs.

The answer is that every option has costs. We've attempted to display the average annual costs for different types of investment products in Exhibit 11.4. You can see from our chart that some products that we think belong in your retirement income plans have no annual cost, while others charge 300 basis points (that is, 3 percent) or more. Now, we want to make sure you understand that although garden-variety life annuities sold by insurance companies do not charge any ongoing management fees and don't have annual management

Exhibit 11.4 The Ongoing Costs to Pensionize

	United States	United Kingdom	Canada	Australia	New Zealand
Single-Premium Income Annuity, Annual Fee	embedded fees—but less than traditional money management fees			mix of embedded and immediate fees	–
Clipping Coupons from a Government Bond, Total Annual Fee	0%	0%	0%	0%	0%
Exchange-Traded Equity Fund, Total Annual Fee	0.5–0.85%	0.1–0.8%	0.5–0.85%	0.1–1.2%	0.5%
Mutual Fund, Total Annual Fee	0.87%	1.13%	1.84%	0.89%	1.75%
High-Equity Variable Annuity with Guaranteed Living Income Benefits, Total Annual Fee	1–4%	1.25–3.5%	3–5%	1.5–4.3%	–
The Cost of Having No Idea What You Are Doing	*infinite*				

Notes: Life and variable annuities are not currently available for purchase in New Zealand. Detailed source information available in the Notes section.

expense ratios, they aren't provided for free as a public service. The insurance company makes some profit on them, in the form of embedded fees, which means that you are paying for this in the form of lower income. However, once the company has committed or promised to make a certain payment to you, they can't reduce your income or increase any fees for the rest of your life. Contrast that with a mutual fund or segregated fund, where every day can be a new (fee) day. This is why we chose to put the number 0 percent in the chart for life annuities, but noted that there is an embedded cost to annuitize.

You may notice that at the bottom of our chart we've included the infinite cost of having no idea what you are doing. For us, this gets at what we think is the heart of the real question about costs—not what the annual costs are, but whether or not you are getting value for the fees you pay.

Don't misunderstand us: we think knowing what your costs are (whether for financial products, financial planning, or both) is an important part of being an informed investor. However, we don't think investment fees are necessarily a bad thing. The question you should ask yourself, in our view, is: "Am I getting what I want from paying these costs, including a retirement income strategy I am satisfied with?"

We would not counsel you to avoid fees or implement the lowest-cost solutions. Instead, our focus is on ensuring you get a retirement income solution that is keyed to your specific RSQ and EFL desires and delivered in a way that works for you. You may want to take a moment to think about the kind of relationship you want with a financial adviser, if you haven't already answered this question for yourself, as well as the process you'd like to follow in working with an adviser to pensionize your nest egg. In order to buy many of the products discussed within this book, a licensed financial adviser will be required. If you're planning your retirement income strategy, you should be picky about this decision and should seek out good credentials and referrals.

HOW TO CHOOSE A FINANCIAL ADVISER

This book is full of concepts, and you may decide you'd like to work with a financial adviser to help apply them to your own personal situation. But how should you choose an adviser?

There are many different types of financial advisers, including *accountants* (who provide you with advice on tax matters and help you prepare and submit your tax returns*), financial planners* (who use the financial planning process to help you figure out how to meet your life goals—typically by looking at all of your needs, including budgeting and saving, taxes, investments, and insurance and retirement planning), *insurance agents* (who are licensed to sell life, health, annuity, and other insurance products), and *investment advisers* (who are compensated to provide securities advice).

Each of these types of advisor has various strengths and areas of expertise. Keep in mind that this book is about retirement income planning, so whichever adviser you choose should have specific expertise in the retirement stage of life (versus the accumulation stage).

In fact, one of our motivations for writing this book was our belief that the deaccumulation stage of life has received inadequate attention from the financial advisory industry. So if you are persuaded by the evidence you're reading in this book and want to work with a financial adviser to pensionize your own nest egg, consider interviewing advisers specifically to evaluate their interest and expertise in creating sustainable lifetime retirement income plans—that is, advisers who can help you define and measure your own wealth-to-needs ratio, and the Retirement Sustainability Quotient and Expected Financial Legacy of your retirement income plans.

When Should You Pensionize?

Other questions you may be asking yourself are, "When should I start the process of pensionizing my nest egg? Is this something I do all at once, or can I get into this slowly, dipping one toe in at a time?"

The answer to all of these questions is that pensionizing is a gradual process that can take place starting as early as 50 or so (if you are thinking about using deferred income annuities) and concluding as late as age 80.

In fact, our reason for giving you a lot of the theoretical concepts we went over in this chapter was to help you understand and time the pensionization process. We've told you that your wealth-to-needs (WtN) ratio will change over time and that your RSQ will change as well. In our view, you should start to look at these issues when you are 10 to 15 years away from your desired retirement age, and think carefully about what steps you want to take first, and when.

For example, we've suggested that if you say, "I'm going to stay fully invested in the stock market until my desired retirement age and then I'm going to annuitize everything," then you would be exposing yourself to a number of different risks. These include the risk that your nest egg will fluctuate downward in value just as you want to buy an annuity, and the risk that annuity prices might be at historical lows. We've also suggested that annuity purchases pay out more if you buy them at advanced ages.

In our view, you should use the concepts we've laid out in this part to help you understand where you sit on the retirement income frontier over time. If you find yourself in a spot that's uncomfortable (with an RSQ or WtN ratio that is too low), use the tools of pensionization to move to someplace with a better fit!

We suggest that you review your RSQ and EFL values periodically, perhaps as often as every year. In addition, if your circumstances change, your RSQ may change as well. One circumstance you may be worried about is if your investments experience a large decline in value before you retire or in early retirement. If you would like to be extra cautious in planning for retirement but before pensionizing, we suggest you run your RSQ calculations with your current assets, and then again assuming a 20 percent drop in value. If your RSQ shifts downward dramatically or unacceptably after a market downturn, you may want to take steps to protect your nest egg from market volatility, such as by purchasing a variable annuity (VA) with a guaranteed living benefit, or other product that provides a guaranteed lifetime income stream. But the underlying point here is that your RSQ can and will change. We're going to give you a tool to run some calculations in Part Three, so stay tuned.

When Should You Turn Your Living Benefit On?

Now, some readers may have a different version of the question "when should I pensionize?" If you have already purchased a product that provides pensionized income, but requires you to "turn on" your living income benefit, how do you know when it's time to flip the switch? (We emphasize that this discussion is for readers who already own a product that can provide guaranteed income for life, but the lifetime hasn't been "switched on" yet.)

Here's our thinking: Recall that the variable annuity with a guaranteed income rider allows you to invest in a diversified portfolio of stocks and bonds, but that you also pay (as we've just reviewed) perhaps 1 to 3 percent extra for a unique insurance policy (a "rider" in insurance industry terms) that allows you to receive guaranteed lifetime income from the portfolio, no matter how well or how poorly the underlying stocks and bonds fare. This rider is worth something to the purchaser for two reasons: first, the probability that the investment account might be depleted by withdrawals at some date, and second, the possibility that you might live beyond that date.

It's important to understand that the insurance premiums you are paying actually come to an end if the value of your underlying investment account hits zero. So, looking at just this issue in isolation, the sooner you can stop those fees, the better—which also means the sooner you can start withdrawals, the better.

But, you may ask, what about the promise of a higher guaranteed base, and thus higher guaranteed withdrawal amounts, if I delay turning on the income from my variable annuity? Our main argument here is that these features, while tempting, are not tempting enough to justify waiting.

We reviewed the basis of this argument in Chapter 6, when we looked at the cost of immediate and deferred annuities, and how the price of annuitized income changes with the age of the purchaser. Remember that you can buy more annuity income with the same dollars if you start your income later. The converse of this statement, however, must be that if you are going to delay taking income from your variable annuity, you must be compensated for waiting.

Let's say you are age 65 and you are wondering whether to turn on your guaranteed living income benefit today, which would provide you with $10,000 per month, or defer for one year (we'll use $10,000 per month because it makes the math easy to understand). You know that if you defer, you may be able to reset the guaranteed amount you receive based on how well markets do. So how much more income should you get (starting at age 66) to adequately compensate you for the income you didn't get (starting at age 65)?

As it turns out, this isn't a question of personal preferences: it is a question that has a straightforward answer that can be calculated using actuarial finance, much like—as we saw earlier—the cost of annuities purchased at various ages can be calculated and known. If you do the math, in this case the breakeven point for delaying income for one year is $10,680. That is, you would need an extra $680 per month for the rest of your life, or 6.8 percent more income, to make up for the lost $120,000 between ages 65 and 66.

Does this mean that you should delay taking income or turn your income benefit on now? Here's how to think about this question, using the example we've provided: If your rider is guaranteeing 6.8 percent more lifetime income for waiting a year, or if you are certain your guaranteed base will grow (after all fees are deducted) by more than 6.8 percent over the next year—then go ahead, wait the year, and reconsider at age 66. But if your answer to either of these questions is "no"—you don't have a rider that guarantees 6.8 percent, and you aren't certain your base will grow by more than 6.8 percent over the coming year—the math says *turn on the income rider now.*

And at age 75, the argument is even more compelling—again, for the same reasons we saw when examining the math of immediate and deferred life annuity prices based on purchase age and age at income start date. At the age of 75, the threshold rate is now 9.4 percent, which is almost impossible to beat even in the most perfect market conditions.

WHEN SHOULD YOU TAKE SOCIAL SECURITY?

In reading this section, you may be wondering whether the concepts we are discussing also apply to the decision about when to take public pensions—such as Social Security retirement benefits in the United States.

However, the decision about when to take public pensions is far beyond the reach of this book, as there are many, many potential permutations and implications from this decision depending on

(continued)

your specific and individual circumstances and preferences (such as whether you are married or single, have children, are planning to take a public pension "early" or "late," and more).

Instead, we recommend you seek out these websites if you are in the United States and you're looking for more information about this aspect of your retirement finances:

- maximizemysocialsecurity.com
- socialsecuritysolutions.com
- "Efficient Retirement Design" at siepr.stanford.edu

All three of these sites have devoted the time and attention to the Social Security decision that this complex issue requires.

Exhibit 11.5 shows the "hurdle rate" for purchasers of varying ages. Note how the rate at age 55 differs from the rate at age 75. You can see that at younger ages, and for accounts that are packed with high-growth assets, there is a reasonably high probability of beating those hurdle rates, but not once you hit your 60s and 70s.

Exhibit 11.5 Guaranteed Size of Birds in Bush Needed to Beat the One in Hand

Current Age (Male)	Guaranteed Lifetime Monthly Income Starting Today . . .	Is Actuarially Equivalent to Income Starting Next Year . . .	This Is a "Hurdle Rate" for the Base of . . .
55	$10,000	$10,539	5.4%
65	$10,000	$10,680	6.8%
75	$10,000	$10,936	9.4%

Keep in mind, however, that every situation is unique, and your variable annuity policy—if you have one—may include other riders and features, such as enhanced guaranteed minimum death benefits or joint-life options that mean the math is more difficult to work through. But at a basic level, our point is that you should understand the cost of delaying and the benefit of turning on your income rider now.

In this chapter, you did most of the heavy lifting to work through the concepts that underlie the argument for pensionizing your nest egg. The basic idea we wanted to explore was that pensionizing—which involves using one of the oldest financial products still in existence, the lifetime payout annuity—increases your retirement income sustainability (which must be traded off against your financial legacy value).

But all of these concepts are introduced from the point of view of someone who is considering pensionizing now. In the final chapter in this part, we are going to activate a time machine and revisit the Two Gertrudes, whom you first met in the Introduction.

12

A Deeper Look at the Promise of Pensionization

Revisiting the Two Gertrudes

Do you remember the two Gertrudes we told you about in the Introduction? Recall that both Gertrudes are 85 years old and in good health, *but Gertrude 1 pensionized part of her nest egg when she hit retirement*, while Gertrude 2 did not. As a result, in the later years of her retirement, the first Gertrude lives a life free of financial worry, while the second Gertrude is haunted by the complex financial decisions she faces with each passing year.

In the Introduction, we asserted that Gertrude 1, with pensionization, is better off than her counterpart. Pretty bold, right? In this chapter, we're going to back up that assertion by looking much more closely at our two Gertrudes—one who pensionized and one who did not. And we're going to point you toward some calculators and tools that will help you delve more deeply into your own situations. (Before we start, we want to advise you to think about this chapter as kind of an "advanced credit" section of the book, because we are going to introduce a number of technical concepts that supported Gertrude's decisions. However, we think these concepts help in understanding the decisions that retirees increasingly need to consider, so we invite you to keep reading!)

When we met both Gertrudes, they were 85, but Gertrude 1 had pensionized part of her nest egg at age 65, twenty years earlier. Gertrude 1 clearly believed that she would be better off by pensionizing. Let's review the conversations she had when she was making her decision.

Activating the Time Machine: Gertrude at Age 65

The first question that Gertrude had when she was considering pensionizing is how she would be better off as a result. How do we answer that question?

Prior to pensionizing, Gertrude's investment portfolio was made up of conventional stocks, bonds, exchange-traded funds (ETFs), and other investment products. These types of products are almost universally measured and compared by their *yield*, or the income return on the investment, usually expressed as an annual percentage. For example, mutual fund yields are an annual percentage measure of the income (dividends and interest) earned by the fund's portfolio, net of the fund's expenses. The use of a universal measure like investment yield allows investors to easily compare investment alternatives.

But how do we measure the yield of an income annuity or other product that pays out as long as the recipient is alive? With a life annuity, the yield goes up with every year in which payments are made, so it starts low (in the early years of payments) and rises over time.

Let's put some numbers around this discussion about annuity yield. In December 2014, a healthy 65-year-old American woman with $100,000 could purchase an income annuity that includes a guaranteed payout for life, with a 10-year guarantee, that would pay her about $525 per month. (The 10-year or "period certain" guarantee means that payments will be made for at least 10 years.) In order to determine the final yield of the $100,000 premium for the life annuity, we'd need to know how long the purchaser will live—and we can't know that in advance.

Let's take a moment to look at this question more deeply. If we start with a large group of healthy 65-year-old women, we can say that, on average, they will live for 25 years. As we saw in Chapter 2, this is known as their life expectancy. But a key reason that Gertrude considered pensionizing is that she knew that she might live longer than the population average, and she wanted peace of mind in knowing that she would receive a paycheck from the income annuity until the day she dies. In other words, the insurance benefit—the guarantee to pay for the rest of her life—was very important to her.

As we saw in Chapter 6, some people will live longer than others and the income annuity is a vehicle that allows those with a shorter life span to subsidize the retirement income of those that will live longer (using the power of mortality credits). To reiterate: no one knows if they will outlive the average or not. The key point is that if the purchaser—you, Gertrude, or anyone—lives longer than average, she increases her risk of depleting her income-generating assets. An income annuity allows you to transfer this risk to an insurance company.

So if Gertrude wants a guarantee of income for life, she will eventually need to consider pensionizing her nest egg, or purchasing an annuity or product that provides guaranteed lifetime income. In this case, we'll use the example of a life annuity as we described in Chapter 6. Should she buy an income annuity now or purchase a different product now in anticipation of buying the annuity at some future date, when it is cheaper because she's older? We can determine the answer to that by looking at a statistic called the implied longevity yield (ILY), which we first mentioned in Chapter 6.

Lifetime Income: Now or Later? The Implied Longevity Yield

Let's assume that Gertrude has carefully worked out her retirement income needs, and knows how much she needs to earn from her investments in order to meet those needs in retirement. Let's also assume that Gertrude is contemplating buying an income annuity, has read with interest our (fictitious) example of Great-Grandma's Poker-Table Bet, and wants to know if she should delay the annuity purchase in order to benefit from increasing mortality credits over time.

Most people have trouble thinking about and planning for the rest of their lives, which can feel very uncertain—so let's add a little bit of certainty by choosing a seven-year planning horizon. Specifically, Gertrude is now wondering whether (a) to purchase the annuity at age 65, or (b) buy an liquid investment that pays the same monthly income as the annuity would for seven years, and then buy the annuity later, when it will be cheaper (that is, it will provide higher monthly income for the same purchase amount). See Exhibit 12.1, which shows these two options as Plan A and Plan B.

Exhibit 12.1 Lifetime Income: Now or Later? Illustrating the Implied Longevity Yield

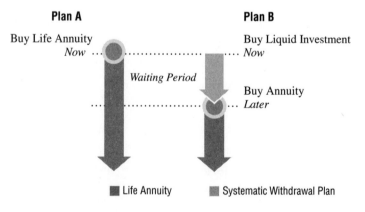

Another way to think about Gertrude's question is: *What yield would she need to earn from a liquid investment that would pay her the same monthly income as an annuity for the next seven years, while also leaving her exactly enough money to purchase the same stream of income seven years from now?*

We can think of this as calculating the implied longevity yield (ILY) of an income annuity. While the math required to answer this question is not straightforward, there is a tool that provides the answer. In this case, Gertrude would need a guaranteed yield (net of commission and expenses) of 4.6 percent from a source that is as financially strong as an insurance company every year for the next seven years to justify waiting those seven years to purchase an income annuity. This is the ILY value for Gertrude at age 65, looking over the next seven years.

Technically, the ILY value is equal to the internal rate of return over a specific waiting period that an individual would have to earn on their investable wealth if they decided to fund their retirement income needs (during the waiting period) by using a systematic withdrawal plan. Here's how to think about the ILY numbers: An ILY that's larger than prevailing yields from other sources indicates a greater relative benefit from immediate annuitization, and also shows the benchmark rate of return the portfolio would need to earn in order to provide the same benefit to the retiree.

How might the ILY calculation be useful to you if you are faced with the same questions as Gertrude was? If you are interested in computing the ILY, applicable today in the United States or Canada for your situation, you can go to the **pensionizeyournestegg.com** website, where you can find more information and an ILY tool. This tool can provide you with some guidance on what your investments must earn if you decide to delay your annuity purchase by a few years. Waiting to pensionize—in the hope of getting better rates later on—runs the risk that your money won't earn enough to generate a periodic income and the lump sum needed to purchase the annuity later on. The ILY calculator will tell you what the threshold or benchmark rate actually is.

This isn't to say that every 65-year-old should buy an income annuity immediately. As we saw in Chapter 9, some people nearing or in retirement are in no real danger of depleting their retirement assets because they have a high wealth-to-needs (WtN) ratio.

Still other people might be sure that interest rates will rise soon, and wonder whether they should delay an annuity purchase in anticipation of rising rates. We touched on the question of how interest rates affect annuity payouts in Chapter 6, when we saw, in the example of Great-Grandma's Poker-Table Bet, that the spread or difference between the investment return from the longevity bet contract and the interest rate earned on the entire fund grows exponentially as Great-Grandma ages (that is, it grows at a rate that becomes ever more rapid in proportion to the total; see Exhibit 6.5 for a refresher on this point.)

If you expect interest rates to rise, or even if you are simply wondering how a change in interest rates might affect annuity payouts, how do you explore the potential impact of rate changes on your pensionizing plans? Now let's look more closely at the relationship between changes in interest rates and annuity payments.

Lifetime Income: Now or Later? The Role of Changing Interest Rates

Earlier in this chapter, we showed how—by using the ILY tool—it can be difficult to beat the return from an income annuity for a 65-year-old purchaser while drawing income from a portfolio and preserving the income-purchasing potential of the portfolio.

However, the ILY tool does not take future changes in interest rates into account. Instead, it assumes that interest rates will not change from their current lows (or, if they have risen by the time you read this, the tool assumes they will remain at those higher rates).

Accordingly, another question that Gertrude had when she was first contemplating pensionizing her nest egg is whether she should delay the purchase if she expects that interest rates will increase in the next few years. And the same goes for you, too—if you think that interest rates will rise in the coming years, does that mean you should wait to pensionize?

In order to answer that question, we first need to explore the relationship between interest rates and annuity payouts. In Chapter 6, we introduced the concept of the "yield curve," which is a graph that illustrates the relationship between yield and maturity among similar fixed-income securities. A normal yield curve is one in which longer-maturity bonds have a higher yield compared to shorter-term bonds, due to the risks associated with time.

Income annuity rates are driven by a yield curve that is similar to long-term corporate bond yields. In the United States, annuity rates are driven by the U.S. Treasury yield curve, which compares U.S. debt of different maturity dates, such as bonds with 1-year, 5-year, and 30-year maturity dates.

Back to Gertrude, at age 65: Her question is, if I am interested in pensionizing a portion of my nest egg to create guaranteed income I can't outlive, but I expect interest rates may rise in the next few years, am I better off waiting to purchase an annuity, or should I buy today?

In order to help Gertrude—and you—answer this question, we will use another innovative tool that helps analyze the decision to pensionize while taking into account the impact of changes in interest rates over time on annuity payout rates. Let's say that Gertrude is considering delaying the purchase of an annuity by five years, until her age 70. And let's further assume, as we did earlier in this chapter, that she's allocated $100,000 of retirement savings to the annuity purchase (whether now or later), and her monthly income—whether from the annuity (a life annuity with a 10-year guarantee, as we explored earlier in this chapter) or using a systematic withdrawal plan—would be the same in both cases at $525.

In mid-2014, the U.S. Treasury was showing a yield curve for 1-, 5-, 10-, and 30-year rates of approximately 0.2 percent, 1.7 percent, 2.4 percent, and 3.1 percent, respectively. (In this example, we'll refer to U.S. rates.) Let's assume that Gertrude chooses to invest in a 5-year Treasury Bill while she's waiting (in order to ensure that the money she intends to use for the annuity purchase is available at the end of 5 years, when she's ready to buy).

Now, in order to compare the yield from an annuity under interest rate conditions that are different than the conditions in mid-2014 we need to choose or assume some different future rates in order to see the impact of these different rates on Gertrude's decision to delay pensionizing (or not). If we are evaluating the impact of interest rate increases on Gertrude's annuity purchase decision, by how much should we assume those rates increase?

In this case, we will assume that Gertrude expects—at least for comparison purposes—that interest rates (as expressed by the U.S. Treasury yield curve) might rise as high as their highest point in the past 10 years. Over the past 10 years, Treasury rates peaked in 2008 at approximately 2.5 percent, 3.75 percent, 4.25 percent, and 4.75 percent for the 1-, 5-, 10-, and 30-year rates. So in 5 years, when Gertrude is ready to purchase, if rates are as favorable as they were at this peak, would Gertrude be better off purchasing now, or waiting and purchasing when her 5 years are up?

A Tool to Help with Your Decision: The "What If I Wait?" Analyzer

Again, as earlier in this chapter, the math required to calculate and compare these two options is difficult, but a tool to calculate these "what if" scenarios is available—and this tool is available to you, too. If you visit **www.pensionizeyournestegg.com**, you can find a (free) tool called simply "What If I Wait?" that will help you evaluate the impact of changes in the yield curve on annuity payouts for specific situations.

Exhibit 12.2 shows the result of a "What If I Wait?" calculation for Gertrude. In this exhibit, you can see that we've put in Gertrude's age and gender, and the guarantee period for the income annuity she's considering. We've also included how much she's considering pensionizing (as the "amount available to annuitize" value), the best monthly income she can expect to receive (if she purchases an income annuity today), her expected return while waiting (the 1.5 percent available on a 5-year fixed-income investment) and we've specified that if she does not purchase the annuity but waits, her monthly withdrawals from her investment portfolio will match the income annuity payments at $525 per month.

What does Exhibit 12.2 and the analysis it contains tell us? Based on the factors and assumptions we've set out in Gertrude's

Exhibit 12.2 What If Gertrude Waits? Analyzing the Annuity Decision

"What if I Wait?" Sample Illustration			
Current Age	65	Expected Return While Waiting	1.50%
Gender	Female	Monthly Withdrawals While Waiting	$525
Guarantee Period (Years)	10	Waiting Period Before Annuity Purchase	60 Months
		Long Term Corporate Bond Rates	Current	Projected
Amount Available to Annuitize	$100,000	1-year	0.25%	2.50%
		5-year	1.50%	3.75%
		10-year	2.50%	4.25%
		30-year	3.50%	4.75%

Best Monthly Income Available Now	$525.00	Projected Monthly Income If You Wait	$518.26

case, we can see that she would be slightly better off buying an annuity now, versus waiting to purchase the annuity later—because the projected monthly income if she waits is lower than the income she can get from an annuity today. (See the calculated result "Projected Monthly Income If You Wait" at the bottom of Exhibit 12.2.)

We can also see that if Gertrude were able to find an investment that is as secure as a guarantee offered by an insurance carrier, flexible enough to allow monthly withdrawals, and pays 2 percent while she waits, she may be slightly better off waiting. We know this because we've assumed that the rate she receives while waiting is 1.5 percent—if she can increase that rate, without taking on risk, she might be better off.

So far in this chapter, we've worked through a couple of calculations that helped Gertrude decide to pensionize when she did: at age 65, versus waiting until age 70 or later. Based on those calculations and the assumptions and factors we used to populate them, it is clear that the yield generated by an income annuity should not deter Gertrude, at age 65, from purchasing an income annuity.

However, we also know that both of those calculations involved considering the concept of the yield of an income annuity, and we fully acknowledge that yield is an intangible concept—it is difficult to value in concrete terms. Although it allows investors to compare investment alternatives, which can be very useful when you are building your retirement nest egg, once you retire, you—and Gertrude—are probably much more interested in tangible concepts like ensuring that you have a large enough check to meet your income needs (versus comparing yields between various financial instruments). That is, the important question is whether your overall strategy will sustainably meet your income needs in retirement, along with your financial legacy goals.

Now, at several points so far in this book, we've said and attempted to demonstrate that adding income annuities or other annuitized products such as a variable annuity with a guaranteed living income benefit to a portfolio—that is, pensionizing your nest egg—increases the sustainability of your retirement income portfolio. And in this chapter we've discussed whether Gertrude should pensionize at age 65 or wait, based on, first, the ILY (with no assumptions about changes in interest rates) and, second, on an analysis that incorporates how changes in interest rates impact annuity payouts. But there's one more set of calculations we want to walk you through because it provides a much more tangible example of how pensionizing can impact the success of a retirement income plan.

Moving Beyond Yield: Understanding the Cost-Benefit Trade-off of Pensionizing Your Nest Egg

First, let's revisit how retirement income is generated in the *absence* of a strategy to pensionize your nest egg. The most common strategy in use today is a systematic withdrawal plan (SWP), which we reviewed in Chapter 7 and then again in Chapter 9. When we are thinking about retirement income plans and moving beyond the intangible concept of yields and yield curves, one question we might consider is whether pensionizing improves (from a financial point of view) the outlook of a SWP that pays 4 percent per year, increasing with inflation.

Let's go back to our example of Gertrude at age 65. Let's suppose that Gertrude has $400,000 in investable assets in a 60 percent (equities)/40 percent (bond) portfolio. She wants to know whether the purchase of a $100,000 income annuity (paying the same $525 per month, or $6,300 per year as in our previous examples) is a financially beneficial choice for her retirement. For the purpose of this example, we will assume that her return from equities will be consistent at 5 percent. We'll also assume that her bonds will yield a consistent 2.5 percent and inflation will run at 1.5 percent.

Now, we know that purchasing an income annuity involves a trade-off, as does purchasing any investment or insurance product. One trade-off is that Gertrude, if she purchases the annuity, has transferred $100,000 of assets to an insurance company. In exchange, *she has also transferred the risk of depleting those assets* to the insurance company because they will pay out as long as she is alive.

Notice that the income annuity pays $6,300 per year, which is substantially more than the $4,000 she would otherwise withdraw from her investment portfolio using a 4 percent SWP. This means that Gertrude can actually spend more in retirement without increasing her risk of depleting assets.

We've created an exhibit that uses the values and assumptions for Gertrude's case. Exhibit 12.3 illustrates the cost-benefit trade-off of using an income annuity to pensionize your nest egg in retirement. Here's how to understand Exhibit 12.3: the line starting at zero (at the bottom left-hand corner, where the x and y axes meet) shows, year by year, the income that Gertrude receives, starting at age 65, all the way to age 100 (with no assumption about how long she might live). This additional amount accumulates with time, as shown by this line.

The line starting at $100,000 and trending downward, in contrast, shows the impact on her estate of Gertrude's annuity purchase. If she lives a short life (only a few years past age 65), then her estate will be less valuable than it would have been had she not purchased the annuity. And as you can see, the longer that Gertrude lives, the smaller the cost to her estate will be for purchasing an income annuity.

Exhibit 12.3 Illustrating the Cost-Benefit Trade-offs of Pensionizing Your Nest Egg

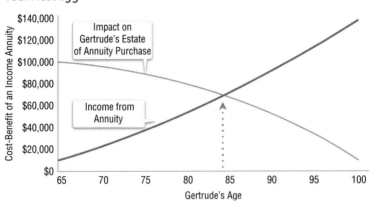

Gertrude's Age

Looking at Exhibit 12.3 as a whole, the distance between the two lines represents the financial benefit (on the right side of the graph) or financial loss (on the left side) from the purchase of the income annuity. Notice that in this case, the two lines meet at about 20 years of retirement. In other words, if Gertrude lives *20 years or more past age 65*, there is a financial benefit to owning the income annuity. Now, as we discussed in Chapter 2, there's no way of predicting how long you will live in retirement. However, we nevertheless have some statistics that can help us think about the probability of living any specified number of years past age 65 (we first encountered these statistics in Chapter 2, where we discussed survival probabilities).

What's Gertrude's chance of living at least 20 years? Statistics tell us that if she is in good health, the likelihood that she will live another 20 years is 68 percent. So, for Gertrude, the decision to pensionize a fraction of her nest egg at retirement was an easy one to make, once she had considered all the elements of her decision: She has a good chance of living to (and beyond) the point at which the income benefit from the annuity is greater than the cost to her nest egg.

In fact, you can see various up-to-date scenarios using this same (free) tool, also available on the **pensionizeyournestegg.com** website. We've called this tool the Pensionize Value Proposition. You'll also need a survival probability calculator to determine what the likelihood of your living to the point where the lines meet in your own case or cases, and we've added a link to that tool on the same site as well.

Pensionizing: Financial and Nonfinancial Benefits

Remember that we said, in the introduction to this book, that Gertrude 1—the Gertrude who pensionized—was better off than Gertrude 2, who did not. And we said at the outset of this chapter that we'd use this chapter to provide some structure and evidence for that assertion.

So how did we do?

In Gertrude 1's case, the choice to pensionize brought with it a number of both financial and nonfinancial benefits. First, the income annuity provided her with a very competitive yield, compared to other products offering similar security and guarantees. However, a far more important financial consideration is whether the decision to pensionize provided Gertrude with the ability to safely withdraw more money from her portfolio. In Gertrude's case, it did. Finally, if Gertrude lives past the age of 85—and she is 85 when we first meet her in the Introduction—she is financially better off as a result of having pensionized at age 65.

There are also nonfinancial considerations to Gertrude's decision. Specifically, in her case (and as we saw in the Introduction to this book), the income benefits from pensionizing, that were guaranteed by a financially strong insurance company, helped provide her with peace of mind and relieved any worry on the part of her children that they might need to support a potentially penniless mother in her old age. Having pensionized a portion of her nest egg, she also doesn't need to worry about maintaining her ability to make financial decisions as she ages. Finally, the reduced need to worry about where her money is going to come from, even if she lives to advanced old age has provided her with a happier retirement. Do you think any of these conditions might apply to you, too? If so, it's time to consider pensionizing your own nest egg, too.

Summary of Part Two

In Part Two, we've looked at human capital, your expected financial legacy (EFL), your Retirement Sustainability Quotient (RSQ), smoothing your lifetime income, your wealth-to-needs ratio, the impact that pensionizing part of your wealth has on the RSQ and EFL, the true value of pensions in pushing the WtN curve higher, and more. We've also explored a set of case studies that demonstrate how you can plot various retirement income plans along the sustainability and legacy frontier, and we've revisited the case of the two Gertrudes to explore the concepts of yield and the cost-benefit analysis of pensionizing. Phew!

As we said, we put you through all of this in an attempt to ensure that you are set up to work through the process of pensionizing your own nest egg effectively—and that's what we'll turn our attention to next.

The Seven Steps to Pensionize
Your Nest Egg

13

Step 1: Identify Your Desired Retirement Income

So far, we've given you a couple of different examples of how to create a retirement income for life, but these exercises have been theoretical. Now it's time to roll up your sleeves and pensionize your own nest egg. We'll start wherever you are now—whether you are 10 years away from leaving the workforce and just starting to think about these issues, or right on the cusp of taking that first step into retirement.

We've created an illustration that shows you each of the steps you will need to take to pensionize your nest egg. Exhibit 13.1 shows you all seven steps together—we will go through each of these steps in turn.

Identifying the amount of yearly income you want in retirement is the very first step in the process of pensionizing your nest egg. Now, some people might think this is the most tedious step because it deals with day-to-day spending and budgeting. However, you just might find that it's the most exciting step because this is the step that is most directly in your control.

Exhibit 13.1 The Seven Steps to Pensionize Your Nest Egg

1 Identify your Desired Retirement Income

2 Calculate your Existing Pensionized Income

3 Determine your Pension Income Gap

4 Calculate your Retirement Sustainability Quotient

5 Assess Your Plan: Is it Sustainable?

6 Calculate Your Expected Financial Legacy

7 Use Product Allocation to Pensionize™
Your Nest Egg

There are two ways to create an estimate of how much money you will need in retirement: working from the top down or from the ground up. The top-down method assumes you'll need some fraction of your working-life income in retirement, so the way to calculate income needs using this method is to slice a portion of your existing pre-retirement income off the top, giving you your desired income in retirement. (Some might refer to your income "replacement rate" in retirement and calculate the amount of income you need in retirement as a percentage of your pre-retirement income. That's what we're describing here.) The ground-up method, in contrast, assumes you will build a budget for your retirement needs by starting at zero and adding up your expenses one by one. We'll work through both of these methods in a moment.

While we were thinking about how you might estimate your expenses in retirement, we took a look at how households in our focus areas currently spend. Exhibit 13.2 provides some of the largest expenses for average households in the five regions where we are focusing our attention.

Exhibit 13.2 Household Spending by Category, All Areas

	United States	United Kingdom	Canada	Australia	New Zealand
Food, beverages, and tobacco	8.9%	12.8%	13.0%	13.5%	20.7%
Clothing and footwear	3.4%	5.9%	4.2%	3.2%	4.1%
Housing, water, electricity, gas, and other fuels	18.8%	25.5%	24.4%	23.8%	24.2%
Furnishings, household equipment, and routine maintenance of the house	4.2%	5.0%	5.5%	4.2%	5.0%
Health	21.1%	1.6%	4.4%	6.2%	2.3%
Transport	10.2%	14.4%	15.3%	10.8%	12.7%
Communications	2.5%	2.1%	2.5%	2.4%	3.1%
Recreation and culture	9.0%	10.7%	8.8%	10.0%	10.4%
Education	2.4%	1.5%	1.5%	4.4%	1.3%
Restaurants and hotels	6.3%	9.9%	7.0%	6.6%	6.1%
Other	13.3%	10.7%	13.4%	15.1%	10.1%

Data for all regions is from 2013.
Source: "Final consumption expenditure of households", OECD.StatExtracts. http://stats.oecd.org (data extracted January 15, 2015).

By the way, you may notice we are talking about household expenses here, not individual expenses. You can use the seven steps outlined in this chapter to pensionize individual or household nest eggs—the steps work for both situations, and it's your choice how you calculate your income needs in retirement. If you are married, you can pensionize your individual nest eggs and then add your eggs together, or you can do the calculations for your household as a whole by adding your nest eggs together first. It's the same nest; you just need to decide—one egg or two? Either way, your omelet has to feed two people.

Back to estimating your expenses. A big item in many household budgets is income tax, which is not shown in our table, and this will likely be reduced at retirement. As you can see from Exhibit 13.2, the biggest consumption expense for average households is shelter-related expenses. If you've planned so that you will be mortgage free at, or early in, retirement, that expense will decrease. (But don't forget you'll still have to heat, insure, maintain, and pay taxes and utility bills for that property!)

Another significant item in the average household's budget is transportation. If part of your transportation costs come from getting yourself to a job and back, you can expect those costs to decrease as well.

Finally, for many households, one of the expense categories while working has likely been putting money aside for retirement, whether in a pension plan or other retirement savings account. This expense will probably end for you at retirement, and you may also downgrade or eliminate any life insurance policies you held while working. Now, you might offset any savings with bigger travel and recreation costs if you plan to "live it up" and increase your overall expenses in retirement—but if you want to use the top-down method, then subtracting a portion of your tax, mortgage, transportation, and retirement savings expenses from your current income is a good place to start in estimating your desired retirement income.

Estimating Your Desired Income from the Top Down

To use this method, you need to determine what fraction of your pre-retirement income you'll need in retirement. But what fraction is appropriate? The target replacement rate is often set at 65 to 75 percent of pre-retirement income for the average worker, while (as we reviewed in Chapter 1) public pensions will usually replace less than 50 percent of pre-retirement earnings for the average worker. So you could just choose an amount between 40 percent and 75 percent of your pre-retirement earnings and stop there. (Lower-income households might require more of their pre-retirement income, closer to 100 percent, while higher-income households may require less, but every household's situation will be different.)

Another top-down way of answering the question "How much income is enough in retirement?" is to simply use your current after-tax income. Yes, make no mistake, you will still have to pay tax in retirement! But for most working people, income tax is their largest yearly expense—and when employment stops at retirement, that big expense is reduced (but not eliminated).

Now, as the financial economist might say, your desired income may be way out of line with your lifetime resources, so don't get too comfortable yet. And one other note before we go any further: we are asking you to estimate your after-tax desired income. That is, the amount of money you want to be able to spend each month, after taxes are paid. (We're going to deal with tax issues in a little more detail as we go along.)

Estimating Your Desired Income from the Ground Up

Another way to get an estimate of your expenses in retirement is to build one from the ground up. This method might take a little more work, but it can give you a good picture of what your current expenses are and how they might change in retirement and, hence, a great target income for retirement planning. To estimate your expenses this way, you will need to review your spending for at least a year. Perhaps you already track your spending year by year. If not, pull out your bank and credit card statements, create a list or table (or even a spreadsheet) of your personal spending categories, and add in your actual expenses.

Once your list is complete, you can estimate what expenses you will retain in retirement, where you want to cut back, and where you want to add. You will need a buffer for unexpected expenses and even upgrades, such as car purchases, gifts to children, charitable donations, and travel. Ultimately, this is an exercise about what you want your life to look like in retirement, and you can get as detailed as you like. Remember, we didn't start out this exercise asking you to identify the bare minimum income you would need in retirement—but the desired income.

Remember, too, there's probably no "right answer" to this exercise! Instead, the goal is for you to create, at least at this point, a starting point for your planning—not a wish-fulfillment or fantasy budget, but a good estimate of your needs plus some "wiggle room" to allow space for you to do things you enjoy and to handle life's unexpected twists and turns.

As we work through the exercise of pensionizing your nest egg, you will almost certainly revisit the first draft you make at this step. Your desired income will also probably change over time as you change your spending habits, or due to the effects of inflation, which we'll explore in a moment, or even due to the life-cycle economic factors we explored earlier. But right now, the goal is to come up with a starting point number you think you can (literally) live with for planning purposes.

Recap of Step 1

- The goal of Step 1 is to estimate your desired after-tax income in retirement. Later, you will learn whether it is feasible.

- You can create an estimate by calculating the fraction of your current working income you will need in retirement (the "top-down" method) or by adding up your expected retirement expenses to get a total (the "ground-up" method).

- Keep in mind that this is a first step in the process of pension-izing your nest egg, and there's no need to get it perfect. You will likely return to this step to refine your estimate later on in the process. So create a place to start and go on to Step 2!

14

Step 2: Estimate Your Existing Pensionized Income

The next step in the process of pensionizing your nest egg is to add up all of your existing pension income.

As we discussed in Part One, practically every retiree in all of the areas we are looking at can count on some pensionized income in retirement. Now, recall what we mean by pensionized income—guaranteed income that lasts for your lifetime. There are two sources of pensionized income you may be able to count on in retirement: the public pension programs broadly available for all retirees and benefits from a workplace defined benefit pension. What sources of pensionized income might you already have? To help you answer this question, this section looks first at public pensions and then at private defined benefit pensions (Exhibit 14.1).

While a comprehensive review of public pension programs is well beyond the scope of this book, this chapter provides some basic information about these programs—plus guidance about where to go for more.

Exhibit 14.1 The Seven Steps to Pensionize Your Nest Egg: Step 2

1 Identify Your Desired Retirement Income

2 Calculate Your Existing Pensionized Income

3 Determine Your Pension Income Gap

Public Pensions in the United States, United Kingdom, Canada, Australia, and New Zealand

Public pensions are meant to provide income to retirees who have contributed, financially and otherwise, to the growth of the country. These income sources are "pre-pensionized" because they are delivered to individuals as lifetime, inflation-adjusted income—you don't need to do anything to pensionize them.

The United States, United Kingdom, Canada, Australia, and New Zealand have public retirement income programs, which replace some fraction of your pre-retirement income. Exhibit 14.2 provides an overview of the gross "replacement rates" that individuals can expect to receive from public pensions in retirement.

How Much Will You Receive?

So how much can you expect to receive in pre-pensionized income in retirement? Just as you estimated your desired retirement income in Step 1, there are a couple of ways to create an estimate, from preparing a rough cut to building a detailed summary. However, unlike estimating your income needs in retirement, in this case we know the maximum amount applicable to each of these sources: the only question is what percentage of the maximum you will receive. In most cases, you should be able to get detailed projections

Exhibit 14.2 How Much in Retirement? Gross Pension Replacement Rates from Public and Mandatory Private Pensions

	Total Public and Mandatory Private Pension Income in Retirement		
	If You Earn 50% of the Median Wage	If You Earn the Median Wage	If You Earn 150% of the Median Wage
	Percentage of Individual Earnings Replaced in Retirement (%)		
United States	49.5	38.3	33.4
United Kingdom	55.2	32.6	22.5
Canada	63.1	39.2	26.1
Australia	91.1	52.3	39.4
New Zealand	81.1	40.6	27.0

Note: Assumes pension eligibility rules and parameters applying in 2012 for workers entering the labor market in 2012 at age 20, and working until the standard pension-eligibility age.
Source: OECD pension models. OECD (2013), *Pensions at a Glance 2013: OECD and G20 Indicators*, OECD Publishing. DOI: 10.1787/pension_glance-2013-en

of your retirement income from public pensions by contacting the responsible government authorities directly.

Benefits from a Defined Benefit Pension Plan

If you have been a member of a defined benefit (DB) pension plan during your working life, you may be eligible for pension income from that plan when you retire. Calculating the amount of income you will receive from a defined benefit pension plan is perhaps the easiest part of the process of pensionizing your nest egg—because for this step all the information is in the hands of other people: you just need to get out and find it.

Note that, as we discussed in Chapter 1 (when we looked at what a pension is), we are dealing only with defined benefit pension plans in this step. While a defined contribution (DC) pension plan is still called a pension plan for statistical and census purposes, it does not provide pensionized income—because there is neither a set amount of pension nor any guarantee about the sustainability of that income over your lifetime. In other words, don't estimate income from a DC plan in this step!

In addition, you may know that when you contribute to a DB pension plan, you can opt not to receive pensionized income from the plan in retirement. Instead, and especially if you leave a plan before you have earned a full pension benefit, you might opt to commute (withdraw) your plan and invest the funds yourself. If you are going to commute benefits from a pension plan (or if you already have), don't estimate any pensionized income from the lump sum you received because there is no guaranteed lifetime income generated from these commuted benefits.

To calculate the pensionized income you will receive from a DB pension plan for which you are now, or once were, a member, contact the pension administrator and ask for an estimate of your pension income at retirement (remember, we're using 65 as a target retirement date right now) from that plan. If you have more than one plan, make sure you get estimates from each one. When you request an estimate from your pension administrator, you may need to answer questions about your anticipated retirement age or years of service for the purpose of calculating your pension benefits.

Note as well whether the benefits include any automatic adjusting for cost-of-living or inflation increases. If your benefits do not include automatic increases over time, we suggest you reduce the estimated total payable by 25 percent for calculation purposes.

What If I'm Worried about the Future of My DB Pension Plan?

After reading Chapter 1, where we discussed DB pension plans reducing or eliminating benefits for retired workers, you may be wondering whether you should somehow incorporate the risk of default for your DB pension plan into your calculations. Here's our thinking: if you suspect or fear your pension plan may reduce or end their payments to you in retirement, leave the plan—if you can (and keep in mind there may be tax implications). That's right, take your money and run. You can build your own pension plan with it. Additionally, if you have reason to believe you need less longevity insurance protection than a DB pension provides, you could commute your pension benefits and take the payout instead.

Note that we are not advocating that civil servants commute their DB pension plans, in part because repurchasing inflation protection would be very expensive, and also because most public servants would not be able to shelter from taxation the full commuted value due to tax limits.

Timing the Retirement Decision

So far, we have not specifically discussed the timing of retirement as a factor in pensionizing your nest egg.

Here's our suggestion: get an estimate of your pension benefits as if you leave the workforce at 65, also known as the "normal retirement age" for many pension and retirement income calculations. While you may retire earlier (or later), part of the work we're doing in these seven steps to pensionize your nest egg will help you make that decision.

Completing Step 2

You are almost done! To complete this step and calculate your existing pensionized income in retirement, simply add your estimates of your public and private pensionized yearly income in retirement.

TA-DA!

Tada! You have now completed Step 2 in the process of pensionizing your nest egg: you have the pretax values for all your pre-pensionized income.

Recap of Step 2

- The goal of Step 2 is to determine the amount of pensionized income you will receive in retirement from public and private sources.

- You can get good estimates of your public pension income from the providers—get in touch with the responsible government agencies for an estimate of your public pension income in retirement.

- Contact the administrators of your current and past DB pension plans for an estimate of your maximum DB pension income in retirement. Make sure to reduce this maximum by 25 percent if the benefit is not indexed to inflation.

- Add up all the yearly income from each of these sources to identify your pre-pensionized, pretax income in retirement. (We'll take tax into account in the next step.)

15

Step 3: Determine Your Pension Income Gap

Now that you've developed estimates of your desired income in retirement and the pre-pensionized income you can expect to receive in retirement, you are ready to calculate your "pension income gap," as you can see in Exhibit 15.1. This is the gap between the income you can expect in retirement and the income you would like in retirement—and you don't need anything more complicated than basic math skills to calculate it.

But before we get to that basic arithmetic, we need to take a moment to consider the impact of taxes on our calculations here. So far, we've only asked you to estimate your desired after-tax income in retirement.

Exhibit 15.1 The Seven Steps to Pensionize Your Nest Egg: Step 3

2 Calculate Your Existing Pensionized Income

3 Determine Your Pension Income Gap

4 Identify Your Desired Retirement Income

Your Average Tax Rate

Let's say you want a certain amount of income each year. You will almost certainly need total income in excess of that amount—because of the income taxes that will be due. Everything you pull out of your tax-sheltered accounts, for example, will be subject to tax because you've never actually paid income tax on that money (for the most part).

Let's start with a very simple example for a hypothetical retiree who has no public pension income and whose entire nest egg is in tax-sheltered accounts. If he has an average income tax rate of 20 percent, then he will have to withdraw $50,000 from his nest egg to end up with a spendable income of $40,000. The rest of the withdrawn funds will go to government in the form of taxes, leaving him with $40,000 that he can consume directly.

In order to figure out how much you will need to withdraw from your portfolio to get the after-tax income you want, the first thing you need to do is estimate your average tax rate. This "average tax rate" simply measures the proportion of your yearly income that you pay as tax. It isn't relevant to your actual tax filing in any year, but tells you the amount and proportion of income you can expect to pay in tax. How do you figure out your average tax rate? You simply divide your total tax paid by your total income. In the case we just examined, we know he paid $10,000 in taxes, and we know his gross income is $50,000. His average tax rate is 20 percent, as 10/50 = 0.2, or 20 percent.

Once you know your average tax rate, you can figure out the gross amount you need to withdraw from your portfolio each year (and you can start to take your public pension and other pre-pensionized income into account, which we will do in a minute). So, if you have no other income, how much do you need to withdraw from your portfolio to get your desired after-tax income? Here's the equation you need to solve:

Gross amount = desired annual income / (1 − average tax rate)

We'll provide a specific example of this equation in the next few pages, so you can see how a "real-life" calculation might work.

A TAXING PROBLEM

As you read our formula for calculating the impact of tax on your pension income gap and spending needs, you may find yourself thinking that in the "real world," tax is much more complex than our simple equation.

Trust us: We don't disagree.

In fact, we believe there is a Nobel Prize in Economics—or Fields Medal in Mathematics—awaiting the scholar or scholars who can derive a formula to accurately and completely calculate the impact of income tax on portfolio withdrawals and spending rates through retirement, while taking into account the multitude of individual circumstances, exceptions, entitlements, claw backs, and shifting rules over time.

So while we know that in an ideal world, we would be able to show you a formula that precisely accounts for all tax factors, we also know that our simple formula provides a basic building block to enable you to think through tax impacts. You can always work on more precise scenarios that apply to your specific situation, perhaps with the help of your local neighborhood tax adviser.

Your Pension Income Gap

Let's work with the $40,000 of desired after-tax income we mentioned a moment ago. Recall that we said our hypothetical retiree needs $50,000 of pretax income to have $40,000 of after-tax income (assuming an average tax rate of 20 percent). Let's continue to assume that all of his funds are in tax-deferred accounts (that is, he has to pay tax on all withdrawals). Now, let's further assume that our hypothetical retiree has $15,000 of pretax public pension income each year.

We just worked out that he has to withdraw $50,000 from his available wealth each year to receive $40,000 in after-tax income.

How does the $15,000 of pension income figure into this requirement? It reduces the amount he has to withdraw to meet his desired income in retirement.

To determine your pension income gap, you subtract the pretax public (or other pensionized) income from the pretax withdrawals you require. In this case, we subtract $15,000 from $50,000 to get $35,000: this is our hypothetical retiree's pension income gap. Recall that this figure measures the gap between the pensionized income you expect in retirement and the income you would like in retirement.

So, what's your pension income gap? Is it positive or negative?

Here are the steps you will need to carry out to calculate your gap:

1. Using the equation we provided, estimate your average tax rate (the ratio of tax paid to total income).

2. Using this rate and your desired after-tax annual income, calculate the gross (before-tax) withdrawals you will need from your retirement portfolio in order to get the after-tax amount you want to receive each year. (In the example we worked through, all wealth is held in tax-deferred funds. If you have a mix of tax-deferred and taxable accounts, your situation will be more complex.)

3. Subtract the pretax, pre-pensionized income you expect to receive in retirement (and added up in Step 2) from the gross withdrawals you need each year.

4. The resulting number is your pension income gap.

If your number is negative, you are done. There is no need for you to pensionize any part of your nest egg—you already have enough pensionized income to meet your daily spending requirements for the rest of your life.

But if yours is a positive number (which we suspect it will be for most people!)—you have a pension gap. What does this mean?

A big number doesn't mean you don't have enough money to retire. Like we said earlier, your pension gap represents the amount of yearly income your personal resources will need to fill each year of your life if you want to maintain the desired income you estimated in Step 1.

Now, you may be thinking, "My number seems pretty large!" But don't panic. This number doesn't represent a shortfall. Instead, it tells you the gap between your existing pensionized retirement income sources and your desired income in retirement. So far, we haven't taken any of your other resources into account. We'll be adding those pieces of the puzzle in the next step, which calculates the overall sustainability (or RSQ) of your retirement income plans.

We suggest you continue to work through the seven steps using the desired income and resulting pension gap you just identified, even if it's large. You can go back to Step 1 and work through the seven steps with a different level of desired income as many times as you like—but we recommend proceeding through the steps with the example you've already started.

Adjusting for Inflation

You may also be thinking, "But the number I calculated as my pension gap is only valid for one year—it's the income I'd want if I was retiring now. In Part One, you emphasized the impact of inflation on retirement income, so shouldn't I be adjusting that number to account for rising prices over time?"

Before we continue, let's clarify how we are thinking about inflation in these calculations. When we asked you (earlier in this part) to estimate your desired income in retirement, we didn't say anything about inflation. In other words, your estimate assumes that today's prices—on which you based your needs—will remain the same throughout your retirement. It assumes that the inflation rate for goods and services will be zero for the next 30 years or so. Rather unrealistic, we're sure you'd agree. True, as we saw in Part One, inflation has hovered around 3 to 4 percent almost every year since 1995—but there is no guarantee that the rate cannot or will not increase. And even at that a very low rate of 3 percent, the cost of living will still double in a little over 20 years, give or take.

Therefore, a better way to deal with long-term planning (given inflation uncertainty) is to budget and state your needs in real, after-inflation terms. Remember our earlier conversation from Part One: think in real terms.

At the same time, you must also project your investment returns in real, after-inflation terms.

Let's explore this in a little more detail. You essentially want to consume "today" dollars for the rest of your life. For example, when you adjust consumption for inflation, that means you will consume your $40,000 of desired income in your 65th year, then $40,000 multiplied by the first year's inflation rate in your 66th year, then $40,000 multiplied by the first and second years' inflation rates in your 67th year, and so on.

However, there is a neat way to keep things in balance. We already know that your public pension income is inflation-adjusted, and we've told you to reduce your expected income from a non-infla-tion-adjusted DB pension plan to account for the lack of inflation protection.

We also know that when you are filling your pension gap, you will be relying on your private investments, and we'll need to think about and estimate what those investments can earn over the long term (and more on that in the next step).

So here's the balancing trick: when we talk about what your investments can earn, we'll look at returns in after-inflation terms as well, to account for the fact that your needs were expressed in the same framework. In this way, we are comparing inflation-adjusted apples (your desired income) to inflation-adjusted apples (your income from investments). (Remember, we've already adjusted your other income sources for inflation.)

We've now reached the end of Step 3, and you've estimated your pension income gap. Next, we'll start to look at how you are going to fill that gap.

Recap of Step 3

- The goal of Step 3 is for you to calculate your yearly pension income gap. In order to do this, you will need to calculate your average tax rate.

- You calculate your pension income gap by subtracting your pretax, pre-pensionized income (from Step 2) from the gross withdrawals required to obtain your desired after-tax income.

- Your resulting pension income gap does not represent a short-fall; it identifies the income gap you need to fill using your other resources.

- We will take the impact of inflation on your desired income into account by expressing the return you expect on your investments in after-inflation terms. More on this in the next step.

16

Step 4: Calculate Your Retirement Sustainability Quotient

As you have probably already surmised from the discussion so far, your pension gap must be closed (or at least lessened) somehow or your retirement spending plans will not be sustainable.

Accordingly, in this step your savings come into play and it is time to include them in your calculations. To do this, add up the current value of all your retirement accounts. Don't include the value of your house, although it is an asset, unless you plan to sell it to provide retirement income.

What Kind of Eggs Do You Have in Your Nest?

Once you've added up the total value of all your investments, the next step is to figure out what kind of eggs you have to draw on in retirement—so we need to calculate your asset allocation. What do we mean by this? As we discussed in Part Two, asset allocation is simply the process of dividing your funds across various broad categories of investment. (We are not actually allocating your assets here; instead, we are just looking at how they are already allocated.)

Again, to keep things simple, we are interested only in dividing your assets into stocks and bonds.

The reason we look at how your assets are grouped in these categories is so we can better predict how your nest egg as a whole may behave in the future. Specifically, bonds have lower and more stable investment returns than stocks (or said precisely the opposite way, stocks have higher expected returns and higher volatility than bonds). Your nest egg stock allocation may be to mutual funds, unit trusts, exchange-traded funds (ETFs), pooled funds, or stocks you hold directly. Similarly, your bond allocation may be to mutual funds, unit trusts, ETFs, or bonds and term deposits you hold directly. You may even have balanced mutual funds, which hold roughly half stocks and half bonds.

You have a choice here: you can calculate the exact asset allocation of your existing resources and project that allocation over your resources at retirement, or you can select an asset allocation you think is reasonable for your assets at retirement.

To keep things simple, we suggest you choose an asset allocation you think will work for you at retirement, whether 50/50, 60/40, or any other allocation. The point here is not so much to perfectly reflect reality or to precisely predict outcomes; it is to build a workable model. When it comes time to make decisions, working through these questions (whether with precise numbers or not) will equip you with the understanding and tools you need.

Filling the Gap

Now that you've added up your nest egg, it's time to look at how to use it to fill your pension gap. How many years of gap can you fill?

Let's work through a simple example. Assuming you are going to retire tomorrow, if you need $50,000 (pretax) per year and your pretax, preexisting pension income is only $20,000, the pension gap of $30,000 must be financed from your nest egg.

Now, if all you have in your nest egg is $30,000, by the process of simple arithmetic you can see that will last you for a year. What will you do for the remaining 20 or 30 years? If all you have is $60,000, then it might last for two years, depending on how the money is invested. And if all you have is $90,000, then this will probably fill the pension gap for about three, or maybe even four years, if you can have your money grow in the meantime. Certainly, after five years there will be no money left to close the pension gap.

But what about if you have $300,000 in your retirement savings accounts? Or $600,000? How long will that last and be able to close the pension gap? Will it last for 10 years or 20 years? What if you enter a bear market and experience a negative sequence of returns (something we explained in Part One) soon after you retire? And even if the money lasts for 20 years, is that long enough, given the evidence for longevity you also saw in Part One?

We don't really know the answers to these questions, but recent advances in financial forecasting can give you a pretty good estimate of whether your nest egg can fill your pension gap for as long as you need. Although the detailed mathematics are beyond this book, there is a (free) tool available on the **pensionizeyournestegg.com** website that can illustrate the Retirement Sustainability Quotient (RSQ) of financial plans like yours. As we said in Chapter 9 when we introduced the RSQ, think of the RSQ as a meteorological forecast for your retirement plans, taking into account that some of your income is already pensionized.

You can use this illustration tool to help you complete Step 4. The tool on the website requires six ingredients. They are:

1. Your age at retirement.

2. Your desired after-tax income (from Step 1).

3. Your preexisting, pretax pension income (from Step 2).

4. Your average tax rate.

5. The current value of your nest egg at retirement, also known as the value of your retirement accounts.

6. The overall asset allocation of your nest egg.

The web tool at **www.pensionizeyournestegg.com** will help you complete Step 4 (as shown in Exhibit 16.1) in the process of pensionizing your own nest egg.

Exhibit 16.1 The Seven Steps to Pensionize Your Nest Egg: Step 4

3 Determine Your Pension Income Gap

4 Calculate Your Retirement Sustainability Quotient

5 Assess Your Plan: Is It Sustainable?

So how do we calculate the RSQ of your retirement income plan? At a very basic level, your RSQ takes into account your pensionized resources and the assets that can be used to provide income in retirement and assesses how sustainable your income stream is likely to be over your lifetime. That is, the RSQ web site tool gives the success rate of various retirement income plans, taking into account age, average tax rate, pre-pensionized income, and other financial resources and their asset allocation.

The output is a number between zero and 100, representing the "degree of success" of various retirement income plans. Here's the first important thing to notice: the larger the number, the better.

But why is a larger number better? Here are some simple, extreme examples that should make sense. If your desired retirement income is exactly equal to your preexisting pension income, then your pension gap is zero and your RSQ is 100 percent (and if your preexisting pension income is greater than your desired retirement income, your RSQ is more than 100 percent!). Likewise, if you have no preexisting pension income (not even public pension income) and you have no nest egg or savings to fall back on (yes, a very hypothetical situation) then your RSQ is zero.

Now, here's the second vital thing to notice about the RSQ calculator: when you add pensionized income, even though you reduce your nest egg to purchase the pension, your overall RSQ increases. We saw this in a more technical way in Part Two.

In fact, if you purchase a life annuity your RSQ will increase. That is, the overall sustainability of your retirement plan increases as the proportion of your desired income is pensionized. More pensionized income means higher sustainability! You saw this in some detail in Part Two, when we looked at the impact of pensionizing 10 to 40 percent of Robert Retiree's hypothetical nest egg.

Now, this calculator (with six factors) is a rather simple one that doesn't account for all the hybrid products out there; it only looks at your asset allocation. For now (in Step 4) you should get to know your existing RSQ without making any changes to your investments or buying any new financial products.

Keep in mind, as well, that the RSQ is not a measure of the adequacy of your retirement income—you established the answer to the question, "How much is enough?" in Step 1. Instead, it is a measure of how sustainable your current plans are, given some critical inputs—your age, your existing financial resources, and how those resources are currently invested.

For now, there are two things to remember:

1. The higher the RSQ, the better.

2. Adding more pensionized income increases your RSQ!

Recap of Step 4

- The goal of Step 4 is to calculate the RSQ of your current plans.

- There are six ingredients required to calculate your RSQ: your age, desired spending, average tax rate, pre-pensionized income in retirement, the value of your nest egg at retirement, and the investment asset allocation of your nest egg.

- The **www.pensionizeyournestegg.com** website includes a tool that can illustrate the RSQ of various retirement income plans.

17

Step 5: Assess Your Plan: Is It Sustainable?

Y ou now have a Retirement Sustainability Quotient (RSQ) number. It could be 45, 78, 94 (touchdown!). But what does it mean, and what do you do with it? What is a good number? What is a bad number? The way to think about measuring the sustainability of your retirement using the RSQ brings us back to considering your odds.

In our view, unless there's only a 5 percent chance of rain, we strongly believe in bringing an umbrella with you on your journey through retirement. That is, unless your RSQ is 95 percent or above, we recommend an umbrella to protect you from fickle markets, the sequence of returns, unpredictable inflation storms, and uncompensated longevity risk—and the umbrella we recommend is product allocation. If you want to be protected in all kinds of weather, then allocate your investable assets (your nest egg) among different investment products to increase your RSQ.

After you've calculated your RSQ—which is Step 5 in the process of pensionizing your nest egg (see Exhibit 17.1)—where do we go next? It depends on your RSQ. If your RSQ is already above 90 or 95, you are pretty much done. There is no need for you to use product allocation to increase the sustainability of your retirement income. You have a pension gap, but your RSQ is sufficiently high that you don't need to take any further steps to secure your retirement income for life. You do, however, need to double-check your inflation and tax assumptions.

Exhibit 17.1 The Seven Steps to Pensionize Your Nest Egg: Step 5

4 Calculate Your Retirement Sustainability Quotient

5 Assess Your Plan: Is It Sustainable?

6 Calculate Your Expected Financial Legacy

However, if your RSQ is somewhere between 50 and 95, continue to our next step, which will show you how to use the power of product allocation to pensionize your nest egg.

And if your RSQ is less than 50, at this point we recommend that you go back to Step 1 and make some tough choices about your existing retirement plan—by choosing to spend less in retirement, rethinking the timing of your retirement decision, or saving more to support your retirement income goals. A financial economist would say that your desired lifestyle far exceeds your lifetime resources.

Now, you may think this advice is too generic and doesn't apply to your situation. We hope we've convinced you, through our discussion of the risks in retirement in Part One, that even the most risk-loving retiree should consider insuring against inflation, longevity, and sequence-of-returns risks. But whatever you do, we hope we've at least awoken you to the risks you face. The point of Step 5 is just to see where you are and what your next step will be. If you are continuing on through the Seven Steps, your next step is to answer the question, "What's it all about—me or the kids?"

Are you ready? Let's continue on to Step 6, considering your financial legacy.

Recap of Step 5

- The goal of Step 5 is to assess your RSQ and figure out your next step. Are you done, going forward to Steps 6 and 7, or going back to Step 1?

- The result of your RSQ will give you the recommended next step.

18

Step 6: Calculate Your Expected Financial Legacy

We are almost done! The last big conversation we need to have before you are set up to pensionize your nest egg is about the trade-off between your income in retirement (when you are alive) and your financial legacy (after you have passed on).

Now, we've gone over the theoretical aspects of this conversation several times already, in Part Two. What you need to do now is figure out the value that you want to leave as a financial legacy, which is Step 6 in the process of pensionizing your nest egg (see Exhibit 18.1). Whatever number it is, you need to identify this amount so you can assess your plans going forward.

Exhibit 18.1 The Seven Steps to Pensionize Your Nest Egg: Step 6

5 Assess Your Plan: Is It Sustainable?

6 Calculate Your Expected Financial Legacy

7 Use Product Allocation to Pensionize™
Your Nest Egg

To complete this step, you need to know if you'd be satisfied with (to use one extreme example) no assets left over at the end of life—or even living on borrowed money—or if you really need and expect to have $100,000, $250,000, or $500,000 left as a legacy. Now, we know that your total legacy may include lots of nonfinancial (in the sense of investable) assets that nonetheless have value, from your grandmother's silverware to the family summer vacation house. For this calculation, we are only taking into account your investable assets.

You don't need to worry about plotting any frontiers on a graph—you just need to know how much of your current assets you'd like to leave behind. The tool at **pensionizeyournestegg.com** can help demonstrate the Retirement Sustainability Quotient (RSQ) and expected financial legacy (EFL) values associated with different retirement income plans.

The answer to this question will really help you evaluate your retirement income plans, including how much to pensionize. We've said already that the frontier is inevitable: you can't avoid it, and instead you should make sure you are comfortable with the place you end up. We will explore this conversation more deeply in the next chapter, which includes a basic case study examining different plans that lead to different spots on the frontier.

Recap of Step 6

- The goal of Step 6 is to figure out what amount you'd like to leave as a financial legacy.

- Once you have that number in mind, you are ready to move on to the final step—using product allocation to pensionize your nest egg.

19

Step 7: Use Product Allocation to Pensionize the Right Fraction of Your Nest Egg

The very last step is to actually pensionize the right fraction of your nest egg by allocating your resources across the three available product silos.

Working through this step—the final step in our seven-step process to pensionize your own nest egg (see Exhibit 19.1)—requires you to bring together much of the thinking we've done so far, including determining your desired expected financial legacy (EFL). Now, there are many factors that will affect how you actually put product allocation into place and many choices and decisions you will need to make.

We'll consider one case study example in detail so you can see how product allocation might work in practice. Along the way, you'll learn how to use the tool on the **pensionizeyournestegg.com** website to estimate your own Retirement Sustainability Quotient (RSQ) and the EFL of your personal retirement income plans. Keep in mind that this case study is intended simply to illustrate some concepts—any real-life situation will be much more complex than this example.

Exhibit 19.1 The Seven Steps to Pensionize Your Nest Egg: Step 7

6 Calculate Your Expected Financial Legacy

7 Use Product Allocation to Pensionize™
Your Nest Egg

Case Study: Jack and Jill Go Up the Hill (to Fetch a Retirement Income Plan)

Let's take the case of Jack, age 69, and Jill, age 67. They are retired, but don't really have a retirement income plan. They have recently learned about the concepts of RSQ and the EFL, and they'd like to know where they sit on the retirement income frontier. (The kids, in particular, want to know more about their mom and dad's EFL!)

We'll look at where Jack and Jill's current retirement plan puts them, at whether they have an RSQ score that works for them, and at steps they might take to improve their sustainability score. Is pensionizing part of their nest egg a wise choice for them?

Jack and Jill have amassed a nest egg worth $850,000 today. All of these assets are sitting inside tax-deferred retirement savings accounts, which means all money will be taxable as income as it is withdrawn. (The calculations they will need to make would be a bit more complicated if they had a mix of taxable and tax-deferred assets, but the underlying idea is the same whether assets are taxable or not.)

In addition, they are going to go through the steps to pensionize their nest egg as if they have one portfolio. In reality, they have a mix of assets, some held by Jill and some by Jack. However, during their marriage they have never considered their assets separately, so they are going to take on this project—pensionizing their nest egg—as a single unit, consistent with how they've handled their finances so far in life.

Step 1: Identify Your Desired Retirement Income

After going through a budgeting exercise, the couple has decided they would like $60,000 annually (approximately) in consumable, real (inflation-adjusted) dollars. Note that this is the amount they would like after tax—they'd like about $5,000 coming into their bank account every month, which they can spend as they please. Truthfully, they didn't spend a lot of time coming up with this number. They know they will review it more closely as they work through the seven steps, so they decided to start with this ballpark amount.

The first big step they need to take is converting their desired yearly after-tax spending to a pretax amount. This will allow them to figure out how much they need to withdraw from their savings each year to provide them with $60,000 to spend. Using a financial calculator and information from their tax returns, they figure their average total tax rate is about 35 percent. (And again, they are estimating a single average rate for both of them, not individual rates that they would apply to different fractions of their nest egg.)

This is a slightly conservative estimate, as they expect their actual tax rate in future years to be a little below 35 percent (so long as they keep making donations to charity and taking advantage of other tax credits and deductions). But they would rather be conservative in their estimates and have a little extra left over than be overly optimistic and find themselves falling short of funds.

In order to determine how many pre-tax dollars they'll need to provide $60,000 after tax (with a 35 percent tax rate), they need to do a little bit of algebra. We went over this earlier, too. Here's the equation they need to solve:

$$\text{Gross amount} = \text{desired annual income} /(1 - \text{tax rate})$$

Here are the specific values for Jack and Jill:

$$\text{Gross amount} = \$60,000/(1 - 0.35)$$

Solving this equation gives them the gross amount of $92,308; this is the amount they need to withdraw from their portfolio each year to get $60,000 in after-tax income. As we said earlier, you can use this simple equation, too, to roughly approximate your required pretax withdrawals to get your desired after-tax income.

Jack and Jill have now completed Step 1, and have estimated the amount of pre- and after-tax income they'd like in retirement.

Step 2: Estimate Your Existing Pensionized Income

Jack and Jill have a total of $17,000 in public pension income. This income is fully taxable, and they have no other pensionized income.

Jack and Jill have now completed Step 2: adding up their existing pensionized income.

Step 3: Determine Your Pension Income Gap

The next step is for the couple to estimate their yearly pension income gap—that is, the gap between the amount they want to spend and the amount of pension income they have coming in each year.

Now, just a moment ago we said that Jack and Jill estimate they will receive a total of $17,000 in pretax public pension income each year, and you'll remember that Jack and Jill have worked out that they need $92,308 of pretax income each year.

So, in order to take these pretax dollars into account in calculating their pension income gap, they subtract the pretax amount of public pension income from the pretax withdrawals required from their portfolio.

This calculation gives them their pension income gap, which is $75,308 (or $92,308 – $17,000). This is the amount of pretax income they must withdraw per year from their retirement savings accounts so that they get the after-tax $60,000 they desire.

Jack and Jill have now completed Step 3: they have calculated their pension income gap.

Step 4: Calculate Your Retirement Sustainability Quotient

The next question Jack and Jill need to consider is whether their plan (to withdraw approximately $75,000 per year from their nest egg) is sustainable, that is, whether it has a sufficiently high RSQ. Remember that we've said the RSQ is a little bit like a weather forecast, and you want to protect yourself against the chance of rain (running out of money) during your expected lifetime.

As we've said, Jack and Jill have a total of $850,000 in tax-deferred retirement savings accounts, split between them. Because we are assuming one tax rate for both of them, it isn't important to sort out who owns the funds for this calculation. The overall asset allocation in their various retirement savings accounts is roughly 60 percent in stocks and 40 percent in bonds. The real (or inflation-adjusted) rate of return they expect on their portfolio is 3.5 percent, which is also called the geometric mean return. (This rate of return reflects our expectations about the financial economy, and these expectations are "baked into" the tool on the **pensionizeyournestegg.com** website.)

Now Jack and Jill have all the information they need to calculate the RSQ of their retirement plan. If they make no changes to their asset or product allocations, how sustainable is their plan to withdraw an inflation-adjusted, pretax income of $75,308 each year? And what's their EFL with this plan?

If Jack and Jill don't pensionize any more of their wealth and simply continue with their current plan, they have an RSQ score of just 37 percent and an EFL of approximately –$430,000. In other words, they might need almost half a million dollars from their kids. These values were calculated by multiplying the 100 percent certainty of their pensionized income by 1 minus the probability of ruin for the rest of their income stream (the portfolio withdrawals of $75,308).

Exhibit 19.2 The Pensionize Your Nest Egg Calculator

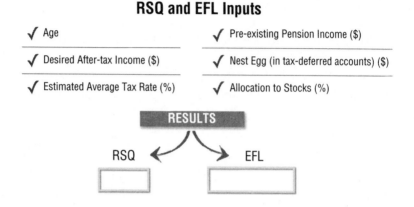

(This explanation may be a little technical, but recall that to calculate the probability that some event will not happen—in this case, the probability that they will not run out of money before they run out of life—we subtract from 1 the probability that it will happen.)

Exhibit 19.2 shows the types of inputs that you will need to see the RSQ and EFL values associated with different retirement income plans when using the tool available on the **pensionizeyournestegg.com** website.

Jack and Jill have now completed Step 4: they have calculated the sustainability and financial legacy of their current plans.

Step 5: Assess Your Plan: Is It Sustainable?

Is that good enough? Both Jack and Jill agree: they aren't willing to proceed any further in retirement with a plan that has a greater than 50 percent chance of failure, and leaves them with a negative expected financial legacy. Instead, they want to explore alternatives to see if they can move their score higher without it decreasing their EFL.

Plan A: Spend Less

There are a couple of different ways they can approach this problem. The first one they want to explore is spending less in retirement. They pull out their financial statements again and take another look at their numbers. After some discussion, they conclude they would be willing to have a stable, inflation-adjusted retirement income of $40,000 after-tax. Sustainability over the long term is more important to them than income in the near term, they agree. (They know they can boost their yearly income by reducing the amount of tax they pay.)

Now their pension income gap has moved from $75,308 to $44,530—due to the effects of tax. Although they have only reduced their after-tax spending by $20,000, the gap has closed by more than $20,000. (By reducing your after-tax spending by $1, you reduce the pre-tax withdrawals from your portfolio by more than $1, as pre-tax withdrawals need to include an additional amount for taxes payable, before the money ends up in your hands.)

Running the calculations again with the revised desired annual income figure, they can see that this choice immediately moves their RSQ to a much more acceptable 79 percent (versus 37 percent with yearly withdrawals of $60,000). It also more moves their expected financial legacy into the black, with a value of $89,500.

However, Jack and Jill are not entirely comfortable with a retirement income plan that still only has a 79 percent chance of success.

Plan B: Pensionize a Fraction of Your Nest Egg by Buying an Annuity

After some more discussion, they decide that, in addition to reducing their spending level, they'll also consider purchasing an annuity. By spending $200,000 today to purchase an annuity, the total size of their nest egg does not change—but more of it is pensionized. Jack and Jill know (from reading this book) that increasing pensionization equals increasing sustainability. By how much does the sustainability of their retirement income plan change if they pensionize more of their nest egg, and what is the impact on their EFL?

Here's the answer they get from their calculations: by using $200,000 to purchase an annuity, they will get $12,800 more in annual, pretax income each year (with an annual 2 percent cost-of-living adjustment). (Note that their annuity income doesn't affect the amount of after-tax income they will receive each year; it just closes their pension income gap.) This in turn moves their sustainability score from 79 percent (mediocre) to 88 percent (much healthier), which is much more acceptable to them. Now their pension income gap is $39,400—less than half of what it was when they began.

Step 6: Calculate Your Expected Financial Legacy

In Plan B, their financial legacy has moved from negative territory (in their original plan) to $140,944. It isn't as high as it would be if they were to reduce spending but did not pensionize any (more) of their nest egg. However, as we have said, and this case study demonstrates, if you want a higher RSQ, you must accept a lower EFL.

Now Jack and Jill have the beginnings of a workable plan. They can see, conceptually, the impact that pensionizing some fraction of their nest egg has on the sustainability and legacy of their retirement income plans. And importantly, they can see that it improves both the sustainability and legacy of their original starting point.

Exhibit 19.3 shows the changes in RSQ, EFL, the percentage of pensionized income, and the pension income gap for each of these three possible plans: their original starting point, Plan A (spend less), and Plan B (spend less and buy an annuity).

Exhibit 19.3 Jack and Jill's Pensionization Process

STARTING POINT		Pension Income Gap (pre-tax)	RSQ	EFL
Nest Egg (pre-tax)	$850,000	$75,308	37%	−$429,428
Plan A Reduce Spending	Reduce desired after-tax income			
Result:	−$20,000	$44,538	79%	$136,386
Plan B Pensionize™	Spend $200,000 on Life Annuity			
Result:	+$12,800	$31,738	88%	$140,944

Step 7: Use Product Allocation to Pensionize Your Nest Egg

Now that they have the basic parameters of a plan set out, Jack and Jill can start to optimize their plan along the retirement income frontier. They can, for example, experiment with pensionizing more of their nest egg. They can also change the asset allocation in their tax-deferred account. In addition, Jack and Jill's paths will vary with their circumstances, needs, and wants.

Jack and Jill may not like the idea of irreversibly pensionizing a fraction of their nest egg using a life annuity. This is where a hybrid retirement income product may come in handy for them—because a hybrid product would allow them to retain the funds in their nest egg while generating pensionized income from those funds. Now, to compute the RSQ for a nest egg allocation that includes products from all three silos is beyond the scope of this book, and you will need to consult with a financial adviser to work through scenarios and plans that include variable annuities. However, it is important to note that this course of action will not increase your RSQ as much as a lifetime payout annuity, but it will provide greater liquidity and a higher EFL.

Summary of Part Three

We have now reached the end of Part Three, and we've worked through one example of how a couple might pensionize their nest egg. We've reviewed each of the steps along the way to pensionization and hope that we've set you up to start to work out your own plans. But more than that, we hope we've opened up some new ways to think about retirement income planning and provided some new strategies to consider as you move forward with this stage of life.

Final Thoughts

Most books on personal finance try to provide comprehensive advice on all aspects of wealth management and investment planning. Chock-full of tips, suggestions, and ideas for helping you improve all the monetary aspects of your life, they aspire to become the encyclopedic go-to location for all things financial.

As you can probably tell, this is not that kind of book. In contrast to most other books about managing your money, we feel quite comfortable summarizing the main idea of this entire book in one simple sentence:

If you won't have income from a real pension in retirement, make sure you go out and get some real pension income.

Everything we said in this book was our attempt to make the case for why this one idea is so important. Along the way, we defined the characteristics of a true pension and challenged you to confirm whether or not you have one. We provided some guidelines for how to determine whether your pension will truly protect your retirement, and we offered some suggestions about modern pension products that can help fill in your pension income gap.

Our motivation for writing this book came from the hundreds of discussions we've had on the topic of retirement income security. Over the years, when we asked people from all walks of life the very basic question, "Are you on track for a secure retirement?," we got two general types of answer. The first kind of response was a sheepish admission: "No, I'm worried, and I should probably be contributing more to my retirement savings account." The second type of response was a more optimistic: "Yes, I will be okay; I am contributing the maximum to my retirement savings accounts."

We believe that both responses are incorrect and alarming. We have probably said this at least half a dozen times so far, and we will say it again one final time: a defined contribution workplace pension plan, tax-deferred or tax-free savings account, a permanent or whole life insurance policy, or any large sum of money in a mutual fund, unit fund, segregated fund, separately managed account or discount brokerage account is not a pension. It has the potential to become a pension only if you convert it into a pension.

A pension is a very specific contract between you and a pension provider. A true pension protects you against risks and guarantees a secure, predictable, inflation-adjusted lifetime income for you and your spouse. No ifs, ands, or buts allowed. Recall that we described the new risks that emerge when you enter retirement, inflation, the longevity risk, and the sequence of returns. *Pensionization*—the process of generating your own pension income using the products available today—is the best shield we know of to protect you against these new risks.

Sure, if you want to wait for politicians and public policy experts to fix the public pension system, then be our guest. And true, there is a group out there that is fully pensionized and doesn't need any more help at all, but they are in the minority. Instead, we believe you should take your retirement income security into your own hands and make sure you have some sort of predictable, longevity-insured income, that is, a true pension.

Currently, you can purchase a personal pension only from an insurance company. They are licensed to sell all sorts of pension-like products that protect against the major risks you will face during retirement and which we've described in this book. Perhaps in the future the relevant legislation will be revised and you will be able to purchase a pension directly, in a bank branch, or maybe from the government finance department. But for right now, we just want to ensure you understand the risks of not using pension products.

How much you pensionize, when you start the process of pensionization, and exactly what type of products you use is up to you (and perhaps your financial advisor). In fact, if you are new to money and finance or just don't enjoy this part of life very much, we strongly urge you to hire an expert and outsource the stress. Moreover, this book was never intended to provide all the answers. We wanted to give you a good place to start, not to tell you where you should end up. Instead of all the answers, our intention was to leave you with one, powerful but simple question: *Do you have a pension, really?*

Notes

Introduction

1. In the Introduction, we said that extensive studies have shown that people with pensionized income are happier than people without. To learn more, take a look at the studies by Panis (2003) and Bender (2004), referenced in the Bibliography.

Chapter 1

1. For information on the contemporary pensions situation in the United States, the United Kingdom, Canada, Australia, and New Zealand, we relied primarily on the detailed "country profiles" in the OECD publication *Pensions at a Glance 2013: OECD and G20 Indicators*, with additional context from *OECD Pensions Outlook 2012*. Both are referenced in the Bibliography.

Detailed source information for this chapter is as follows:

- Information on the proportion of U.S. private sector workers with an employer-sponsored pension is taken from "FAQs About Benefits—Retirement Issues," on the Employee Benefits Research Institute website at www.ebri.org/, accessed January 15, 2015. The remainder of information in this chapter on workplace pensions in the United States is taken from U.S. Department of Labor,

Employee Benefits Security Administration, "Private Pension Plan Bulletin Historical Tables and Graphs," published on December 12, 2014 and available at www.dol.gov/ebsa/pdf/historicaltables.pdf.

- Information on the proportion of U.K. workers enrolled in workplace pensions is taken from Snowdon, Graham. "Membership of workplace pensions falls below 50 percent for first time." The Guardian, 24 February 2012. All other information in this chapter on U.K. pension enrollment is taken from The Office for National Statistics, Occupational Pension Schemes Survey, 2013, available at www.ons.gov.uk.

- Information in this chapter on Canadian workers and workplace pensions is taken from Office of the Chief Actuary, "Registered Pension Plan (RPP) and Retirement Savings Coverage (Canada)," available at the website of the Office of the Superintendent of Financial Institutions at www.osfi-bsif.gc.ca, accessed January 15, 2015. Information on Canadians' retirement readiness is taken from McKinsey & Company, Building on Canada's Strong Retirement Readiness, noted in the Bibliography.

- Information on the number of pension plans in Australia before and after superannuation was introduced is taken directly from Australian Prudential Regulation Authority (APRA), Statistics: Annual Superannuation Bulletin, Sydney, 2011. See www.apra.gov.au/ Other information on Australian pensions in this chapter is taken from the OECD publication *Pensions at a Glance*, noted above, and from *The Decline of the Traditional Pension*, noted in the Bibliography.

- Information on workplace pension plans in New Zealand is taken directly from the OECD publication Pensions at a Glance, noted above; including the Country Profile for New Zealand in this publication.

2. To read more about life-cycle thinking and the utility value of pensions, go to the classic work by Modigliani (1986) and the more recent book by Burns and Kotlikoff (2008), listed in the Bibliography.

Chapter 2

1. Information on the health benefits of the Mediterranean diet is taken from Bakalor, Nicholas, "Mediterranean Diet is Good for your DNA." *New York Times*, 2 December 2014.

2. In Chapter 2 and throughout the book, estimates of longevity probabilities were calculated using official life tables for the United States, the United Kingdom, Canada, Australia, and New Zealand as follows:

United States	Male	2009 Life Tables: www.cdc.gov/nchs/data/nvsr/nvsr62/nvsr62_07.pdf (Table 2)
	Female	www.cdc.gov/nchs/data/nvsr/nvsr62/nvsr62_07.pdf (Table 3)
United Kingdom	Male & Female	2009–2011 Life Tables: www.ons.gov.uk/ons/taxonomy
Canada	Male	2009–2011 Life Tables: www.statcan.gc.ca/pub/84-537-x/2013005/tbl/tbl1a-eng.htm
	Female	www.statcan.gc.ca/pub/84-537-x/2013005/tbl/tbl1b-eng.htm
Australia	Male & Female	2009–2011 Life Tables: www.abs.gov.au/AUSSTATS
New Zealand	Male & Female	2009–2012 Life Tables: www.stats.govt.nz/browse_for_stats/health/life_expectancy

Annuity and pension payout rates were calculated using slightly more optimistic longevity assumptions, also known as the RP2000 mortality tables.

Chapter 4

1. All data about current and past inflation rates was sourced from "Inflation, consumer price (annual %)". The World Bank, International Monetary Fund, Inflation and Financial Statistics and data files: http://data.worldbank.org/indicator/FP.CPI.TOTL.ZG/countries/ (accessed January 15, 2015).

Note: Data for the United Kingdom for the period 1965–1988 is the Retail Price Index (RPI), not the Consumer Price Index. In the period 1965–1988 the U.K. government used RPI as the official inflation indicator. RPI data for the period 1965–1988 was obtained from "Annual Abstract of Statistics," 2001 edition. Office for National Statistics. www.ons.gov.uk (accessed January 15, 2015).

2. The "personal inflation calculator" for the United Kingdom is available at www.neighbourhood.statistics.gov.uk/HTMLDocs/dvc14.

See also the 2009 reforms in Australia that introduced a new cost of living indicator, the Pensioner and Beneficiary Living Cost Index (PBLCI), to better reflect price changes facing pensioners.

Chapter 6

1. You can read more about one example of the reaction of pensioners when asked to switch from DB to DC pension plans in the article by Milevsky and Promislow (2004), "Florida's Pension Election: From Defined Benefit to Defined Contribution and Back Again." See the Bibliography for the full reference.

Chapter 9

1. For Exhibit 9.2: Nest Eggs, Pensionization, and Your RSQ, we assumed a 60-year-old unisex retiree who received $2 of lifetime income for $33.33.

We assumed that investable wealth at retirement was allocated to a diversified portfolio consisting of 60 percent stocks and 40 percent bonds. The stocks are expected to earn approximately 8 percent real after-inflation (and after management fees) returns, but with a variability of plus/minus 18 percent.

We also assumed that the inflation-adjusted yield on long-term bonds was approximately 2 percent, again, after all fees.

All of this implies that a diversified 60/40 portfolio of stocks and bonds should grow (using the geometric mean) by approximately 3.5 percent in real terms, with a variability of approximately 11.3 percent per year.

Finally, we assumed that the inflation-adjusted life annuity embedded within this example was priced off the 2 percent real yield, and assuming a mortality model that implies a 5 percent probability of survival to age 100 and an exponentially declining survival rate. We did not assume population mortality rates for annuity pricing and RSQ calculations.

Chapter 11

1. The estimates of mutual fund fees for Exhibit 11.3: The Ongoing Costs to Pensionize is drawn from the study on mutual fund fees around the world by Khorana et al. (2007), and the Morningstar study of Global Fund Investor Experience by Rekenthaler et al. (2013). See the Bibliography for complete information on these sources. All other fee estimates are based on prevailing costs in mid-2014 and were sourced from a sample of publicly-available product prospectus documents.

2. Note that we have focused on ongoing management fees only, and are not implying in any way, shape, or form that immediate annuities are costless or provided on a pro-bono basis by the insurance company.

3. For more information on the experts providing guidance on the Social Security decision in the United States, you can visit:
   - www.maximizemysocialsecurity.com (associated with Laurence Kotlikoff)
   - www.socialsecuritysoltuions.com (associated with William Reichenstein)

     The policy brief "Efficient Retirement Design: Combining Private Assets And Social Security To Maximize Retirement Resources," published by John Shoven and Sita N. Slavov in March 2013 is also available from the Stanford Institution for Economic Policy Research at www.siepr.stanford.edu.

Chapter 15

1. As throughout the book, the calculator noted in Chapter 15 is built on the following assumptions:
   - A Gompertz approximation to mortality
   - A risk-free rate of 1 percent
   - Equity returns of 8 percent and volatility of 16 percent.

     These factors are subject to change without notice. Any future changes to these assumptions will be noted on the calculator itself.

Bibliography

Bender, Keith A. "The Well-Being of Retirees: Evidence Using Subjective Data." Boston: Center for Retirement Research at Boston College, October 2004.

Bodie, Zvi, and Michael J. Clowes. *Worry-Free Investing: A Safe Approach to Achieving Your Lifetime Financial Goals.* Upper Saddle River, NJ: Financial Times Prentice Hall, Pearson Education Inc., 2003.

Burns, Scott, and Laurence J. Kotlikoff. *Spend 'Til the End: Raising Your Living Standard in Today's Economy and When You Retire.* New York: Simon & Schuster, 2010.

Khorana, Ajay, Henri Servaes, and Peter Tufano. "Mutual Funds Fees Around the World." HBS Finance Working Paper No. 901023, July 23, 2007.

Ibbotson, Roger G., Moshe A. Milevsky, Peng Chen, and Kevin X. Zhu. *"Lifetime Financial Advice: Human Capital, Asset Allocation, and Insurance."* The Research Foundation of CFA Institute, 2007.

Mackenzie, George A. (Sandy). *The Decline of the Traditional Pension: A Comparative Study of Threats to Retirement Security.* New York: Cambridge University Press, 2010.

McKinsey & Company, Financial Services Practice. "Building on Canada's Strong Retirement Readiness." February 2015.

Milevsky, Moshe A., and S.D. Promislow. "Florida's Pension Election: From Defined Benefit to Defined Contribution and Back." *Journal of Risk and Insurance,* Vol. 71, no. 3, 2004: 381–404.

Modigliani, Franco. "Life Cycle, Individual Thrift, and the Wealth of Nations." *American Economic Review,* American Economic Association, vol. 76, no. 3, June 1986: 297–313.

Organization for Economic Co-operation and Development. *OECD Pensions Outlook 2012.* OECD Publishing, 2012.

—. *Pensions at a Glance 2013: OECD and G20 Indicators.* OECD Publishing, 2013.

—. *Private Pensions: OECD Classification and Glossary.* OECD Publishing, 2005.

Panis, Constantijn W.A. "Annuities and Retirement Satisfaction." The RAND Corporation. Labor and Population Program, Working Paper Series 03–17. April 2003.

Reichenstein, William. "Calculating Asset Allocation." *The Journal of Wealth Management,* Fall 2000.

Rekenthaler, John, Benjamin N. Alpert, and Sana Suh. "Global Fund Investor Experience." *Morningstar Fund Research,* May 2013.

Acknowledgments

The authors would like to acknowledge the technical support of Simon Dabrowski, Branislav Nikolic, and Faisal Habib of the QWeMA Group, a division of CANNEX Financial Exchanges; as well as Joanne Lui and Jim Dobler of CANNEX Financial Exchanges. Thanks are also due to Lowell Aronoff, CEO of CANNEX Financial Exchanges, and Gary Baker, president of the U.S. Division of CANNEX Financial Exchanges.

Thanks are also due to Warren Huska for illustration and graphics support and to Edna Diena Milevsky for her constructive contributions throughout the lifetime of this project.

Despite the wide array of readers who participated in shaping the first and second editions of this manuscript, the authors alone retain responsibility for and apologize in advance for any undiscovered errors and omissions.

About the Authors

Moshe A. Milevsky, PhD, is an author, researcher, and professor at York University in Toronto, Canada.

Alexandra C. Macqueen, CFP, is a Certified Financial Planner professional in Toronto, Canada.

Index